TLS £7·00

Reflections of a Physicist

ANATOLE ABRAGAM

Reflections of a Physicist

Clarendon Press · Oxford · 1986

Hermann, publishers in arts and science

Oxford University Press, Walton Street, Oxford OX2 6DP
Oxford New York Toronto
Delhi Bombay Calcutta Madras Karachi
Kuala Lumpur Singapore Hong Kong Tokyo
Nairobi Dar es Salaam Cape Town
Melbourne Auckland
and associated companies in
Beirut Berlin Ibadan Mexico City Nicosia

Oxford is a trade mark of Oxford University Press

Published in the United States
by Oxford University Press, New York

British Library Cataloguing in Publication Data
Abragam, A.
Reflections of a physicist.
1. Science
I. Title   II. Réflexions d'un physicien. English
500   Q158.5
ISBN 0-19-851964-8

Library of Congress Cataloging-in-Publication Data
Abragam, A.
Reflections of a physicist.
Translation of : Réflexions d'un physicien.
1. Physics—Addresses, essays, lectures.
2. Science—Addresses, essays, lectures.   3. Research—
Addresses, essays, lectures.   4. Physicists—
Biography—Addresses, essays, lectures.   I. Title
QC71.A27 1986   530'.092'4 [B]   85-21446
ISBN 0-19-851964-8 (pbk.)

French language edition © 1983 Hermann, Paris, France.

English language edition © 1986 Oxford University Press

Printed in France.

Table of Contents

Preface

In the course of my career I have written textbooks and scientific articles directed towards a relatively restricted circle of specialists.

However on several occasions I have had to address less specialized audiences on more general subjects or in less technical language.

Pierre Berès, whose job it is to know about these matters, felt that these fleeting words, which represent the preoccupations of a scientific director and teacher as well as a research scientist, could be of interest to a wider public than the original audiences, hence this collection of essays.

There is one exception; the second text was specially written as a follow-up to the first, twenty years later. Together they constitute an overview of a discipline to which I have devoted a large part of my active life. It reminds me of the story of the little girl who was given a book about penguins. "This book" she complained, "tells me more about penguins than I would wish to know." Readers who are not particularly interested in the recent progress in nuclear magnetism might well wish to skip this second chapter.

I have added to this collection three sketches of great physicists, dear friends now gone, together with a few letters, echoes of remarks made here and there in the various chapters.

A. A.

FOREWORD BY THE TRANSLATOR

Reviewing in *Nature*, *Réflexions d'un physicien* by Professor Abragam, Sir Nevill Mott says: "his French is a joy to read", so it was with considerable trepidation that I undertook this translation. Professor Abragam saved me from the trap of retranslating back into English those sections ("Big Science" and "Doubts and Certitudes") that were originally written in English, sparing me the embarrassement of transforming "Out of sight, out of mind" into "The blind man and the lunatic".

This work is offered in recognition of his great kindness to me when I was a young and very inexperienced research worker in his laboratory at Saclay, many years ago.

Ray Freeman
Oxford, April 1985

FOREWORD BY THE AUTHOR

I wish to express my deep gratitude to my friend Dr. Ray Freeman F.R.S. for accepting to take time from his beautiful research work to do this translation. My only excuse for taking advantage of his kindness is that, being one of the world experts in nuclear magnetism, a key subject of this book, and also bilingual in English and French, there was, quite literally, no one better equipped for the task.

I would also like to thank the Oxford University Press, which over a quarter of a century has provided a nest for my weightier off-springs, for taking under its wing this late and puny child.

A. Abragam
Paris, May 1985

Nuclear Magnetism

I. THE EARLY YEARS *

Fifteen years have gone by since the first nuclear magnetic resonance signals were observed in condensed matter. The circumstances surrounding this discovery are quite remarkable. Two American laboratories, one on the East Coast at Harvard, the other on the West Coast at Stanford, working entirely independently, simultaneously detected the NMR response of protons in paraffin and water respectively. The two groups even used different terminologies to describe these discoveries; the Harvard group borrowed the vocabulary of optical spectroscopy, claiming that they were detecting the absorption by the nuclear magnetic moments of photons of electromagnetic energy of very long wavelength, while the Stanford group, using the terminology of the electrical engineer, declared that they were observing the electromotive force induced in a coil by the forced precession of the nuclear magnetization. The instrumentation that was used and the shape of the signals observed were both quite different.

For months and even years afterwards, according to whether a physicist spoke of nuclear magnetic absorption or nuclear induction, one could decide whether he came from New England or California, more surely than by his accent. The situation was reminiscent of that following the birth of the quantum theory when the devotees of the de Broglie and Schrödinger wave mechanics appeared to be speaking a different language from those

---

* Inaugural Lecture at the *Collège de France*, 5 December 1960.

who followed the matrix algebra of Born and Heisenberg. And just as the adherents of these two theories came finally to the realization that they were really only two different formulations of the same more general theory, quantum mechanics, the champions of nuclear induction and nuclear absorption came to appreciate that these were merely two different aspects of the same phenomenon, now generally if not universally known as nuclear magnetism.

In 1952 the Nobel prize rewarded the work of Felix Bloch and Edward Purcell, the leaders of the Stanford and Harvard research groups. In the fifteen years since that discovery nearly 2 000 publications — on average one every three days — have appeared on the subject of nuclear magnetism. Today the *Collège de France* has a professorial chair devoted to these studies.

What then is nuclear magnetism?

We know now that all matter is made up of electrons and nuclei. Magnetism, as it has been known until now (and is still known) is an electronic property, and perhaps should now be called electron magnetism, nuclear magnetism being due to the atomic nucleus as its name indicates. The concept that the magnetic properties of a substance are the result of the presence within the material of small magnets or individual magnetic moments, can be traced back to Ampère. It is not my task here to evoke the fascinating story of magnetism in which so many seminal contributions have been made by French scientists, Pierre Curie, Paul Langevin, Pierre Weiss, Aimé Cotton, and today Louis Néel, to mention only the modern work. I would like, nevertheless, to outline the guiding principles of Langevin's theory of paramagnetism, which is directly applicable to nuclear magnetism, in the form presented in 1905 in an article of admirable penetration and clarity.

When a sample of material containing elementary magnetic moments is placed in a magnetic field H, such as that existing in the gap of an electromagnet, each of these moments which originally had a random orientation, tends to align itself parallel to the field since this is its condition of lowest energy and hence highest stability. At least this is what they would do if not subject to the competing effect of the thermal agitation within the sample, made evident by the disordered movements of the atoms and molecules which carry the elementary magnetic moments. The effect of the magnetic field is to try to align all the moments along its axis, while thermal agitation favours disorder, so a compromise solution is achieved where the preferential orientation along the field is only partial. If μ is the value of the elementary magnetic moment, and N the number of such moments within the sample, the total magnetization will not be the ideal value $N\mu$ corresponding to perfect alignment, but a smaller value $N\mu P$ where P is a factor less than unity, that could be designated the polarization of the elementary moments. We can appreciate that the degree of orientation would be larger the greater the coupling between the magnetic moment and the external field, and the weaker the effect of thermal agitation, that is to say the lower the absolute temperature of the sample. To a first approximation, P may be taken to be proportional to the strength of the magnetic coupling μH and inversely proportional to the temperature T. In the case of nuclear moments this polarization is always a very small fraction, of the order of 10^{-6} at room temperature and 10^{-4} at the temperature of liquid helium. The magnetization will also be inversely proportional to temperature (the famous Curie law) and will be parallel to the applied field H and proportional to it, a characteristic property of the so-called paramagnetic materials; moreover it will be proportional to the *square* of the strength of the elementary magnetic moment. We shall see later that this was the reason why nuclear magnetism was only discovered at a relatively late date. This approximate law, valid for moderate fields and relatively high temperatures, is only a special case of the general formula established by Langevin, but it is sufficiently precise for a qualitative discussion. In 1905, before the advent of quantum mechanics, Langevin assumed that the magnetic moments could assume any of a continuous range of possible orientations with respect to the magnetic field. Quantum mechanics teaches us that a magnetic moment is associated with angular momentum which is itself quantized in units of $(h/2\pi)$ where h is Planck's constant, and may only take on values of I which are integral or half-integral. There are only $(2I + 1)$ discreet orientations allowed for this moment with respect to the magnetic field direction. In particular, for the smallest non-zero value of I, that is to say $I = 1/2$, only two possible orientations of the moment are allowed, parallel and antiparallel to the field direction. Polarization is complete if all the moments are parallel and zero if there are just as many in each orientation; in the intermediate case the polarization is proportional to the excess of moments in one orientation over those in the other. The requisite modifications of the Langevin result to take account of these quantization effects of elementary moments are rather slight; they were carried out by Léon Brillouin.

A remarkable feature of Langevin's calculation, not always clearly brought out, is that despite appearances and although it dates from 1905, well before the Bohr theory of electron orbits and the new quantum mechanics, it is basically a quantum treatment. Langevin assumes from the start that each atom or molecule making up the sample possesses an individuel magnetic moment μ, and by applying the rules of statistical mechanics, calculates the macroscopic magnetization of the sample based on this simple hypothesis.

A rigourous classical treatment of the electron magnetization from first principles would have expressed the magnetic moment of the atom or molecule as a function of the positions and velocities of the constituent electrons. If this procedure is adopted before applying the Langevin treatment, the magnetization of the sample turns out to have an interesting value: zero. The existence of paramagnetism is incompatible with classical mechanics and classical electromagnetism. It is the very concept of an elementary magnetic moment for each molecule which gives the Langevin theory an implicit quantum mechanical basis.

About half of the stable atomic nuclei, of which there are several hundred known today, possess a non-zero angular momentum or spin in their ground state. With this goes an associated nuclear magnetic moment, parallel in orientation and proportional in intensity, with a proportionality constant γ called the magnetogyric ratio, a characteristic constant for the nucleus under consideration. Nuclear moments are about a thousand to ten thousand times weaker than electronic moments of atoms and molecules. It follows immediately from the Langevin formula that the macroscopic nuclear magnetization of a sample, proportional to the square of the elementary moment, will be in general several millions of times weaker than the magnetization of a paramagnetic substance. Nuclear magnetism is an incredibly weak phenomenon when compared with electron magnetism, and the corresponding experimental techniques are applicable to nuclei only with considerable difficulty. Nevertheless, as long ago as 1937, in an experiment that was amazing for the time, two Russian scientists, Lazarew and Shubnikov, were able to demonstrate the nuclear magnetization of protons in solid hydrogen by a classic measurement of magnetic susceptibility. Despite having stacked all the cards in their favour by working with protons, which have the strongest nuclear moments, at the very low temperature of 2K in order to increase the sample polarization according to the Curie law, this experiment has never been followed up, and there are good reasons to believe that nuclear magnetism would have remained a mere scientific curiosity, if new experimental methods had not been perfected, the technique of resonance.

The principle of resonance, which pervades the field of mechanics and physics, can be formulated as follows: when an oscillatory system possesses a characteristic frequency ω_0, that is to say, when suitably excited and then left to move freely it is capable of a periodic oscillation at that frequency, its reaction (or *response*) to an external periodic perturbation at a frequency ω, is particularly intense when ω is in the neighbourhood of ω_0. Everyone knows the example of the child's swing or the church bell, where repeated pushes, even though weak, may build up an oscillation of large amplitude if the pushes are applied at the right cadence. Another example is that of soldiers crossing a bridge; marching in step they can induce dangerous oscillations in the bridge, but it might be important whether they were at a slow march or at the double. A less trivial example is that of a tuned circuit in a radio supplied with an alternating voltage.

Because the nuclear magnetic moment is colinear with its angular momentum vector, a simple calculation shows that if it is placed in a magnetic field it will describe a precessional motion about the direction of the field with an angular frequency $\omega_0 = \gamma H$, the so-called Larmor frequency. This is in fact the natural frequency of the nuclear spin considered as a resonant system. In a macroscopic sample containing a large number of identical nuclear spins, because the equations of motion are linear, the macroscopic nuclear magnetization naturally possesses the same resonance frequency. At thermal equilibrium, the nuclear magnetization is parallel to the applied field and the amplitude of its precessional motion is zero. It is analogous to a spinning top before it begins to run down. If we superimpose on the static field H an alternating field H_1 at right angles, much weaker than H (for example 10 milligauss in amplitude compared with say 10 kilogauss for H), the effect of this perturbation on the nuclear magnetization will be entirely negligible unless its frequency ω is in the immediate proximity of ω_0. In contrast, if we make ω equal to ω_0, the resonance effect moves the nuclear magnetization away from its equilibrium position along H, causing it to execute a forced precession of finite amplitude. A voltage may then be induced by this magnetization in a coil wound perpendicular to H allowing the resonance condition to be detected. If the frequency of the oscillating field is known for the exact resonance condition this gives the Larmor frequency $\omega_0 = \gamma H$, that is to say the product of the field strength and the magnetogyric ratio of the nucleus in question.

We have treated this phenomenon as one of nuclear induction, in the vocabulary of Stanford. It may be reformulated in the language of Harvard. Take for simplicity the case of spin 1/2 nuclei such as the protons in a sample of water. In a magnetic field, such a spin possesses two quantum states, one parallel and one antiparallel to the field direction, having an energy separation Δ equal to the energy required to flip over the nuclear moment in the applied magnetic field. This energy Δ corresponds, by way of the Bohr condition $\Delta = h\omega_0/2\pi$, to a particular frequency which is easily shown to be the Larmor fequency. In the language of quantum theory, an alternating magnetic field of frequency ω is a coherent ensemble of photons of energy $h\omega/2\pi$. When this frequency is equal to the Larmor frequency, a nuclear spin can make a transition between its two energy states by absorbing or emitting a photon of energy $h\omega/2\pi$, and the resonance condition $\omega = \omega_0$ becomes simply the condition for conservation of energy. Absorption by the spin system of electromagnetic energy stored in the alternating field H_1 affects the transmitter that produces this field and can be detected by standard radiofrequency techniques.

A typical nuclear magnetic resonance experiment would be performed as follows: an electromagnet produces a static field H of the order of several thousand gauss, a radiofrequency coil placed in the pole gap generates an alternating field H_1 near to the Larmor frequency; this coil surrounds the sample under investigation, for example a test-tube full of some liquid. Suitable radiofrequency circuitry feeds alternating current into the coil and detects the absorption of radiofrequency energy by the nuclear spins as the resonance condition is traversed.

Depending on the intensity of the applied static field and the species of nucleus under investigation, the Larmor frequency can vary over a wide range. With magnetic fields of several kilogauss currently in use in laboratories, this frequency is in the megacycle band for most nuclei, that is to say similar to the frequencies used for radio transmissions.

An interesting feature of nuclear resonance is that it is extremely sharp; in particularly favourable cases the resonance width is less than one billionth of the frequency itself. What this means is that a variation of the excitation frequency by as little as one part in 10^9 changes the nuclear spin response significantly, and it is therefore feasible to separate two lines which differ in frequency by less than one billionth of the frequency of one of the lines. To get an idea of what this means, an optical telescope with a similar resolving power would allow a terrestrial observer to separate the two ears of a cat sitting on the moon.

One can therefore appreciate the severe requirements for spatial homogeneity and temporal stability placed on the magnet which generates the static field, as well as the frequency stability demanded of the radiofrequency source.

A point worth emphasizing here is that the magnetic resonance phenomenon is made up of two distinct aspects, the *excitation* of resonance, which involves inducing a transition between two quantum states of the system (for example between parallel and antiparallel orientations of a proton spin with respect to the direction of the field) and the *detection* of the resonance which involves observing that the transition has in fact taken place. It is in this sense that the methods discovered by Bloch and Purcell, which for detection make use of the magnetic properties of nuclear moments, differ in a fundamental way from the other methods of magnetic resonance such as the molecular beams technique used by Rabi before the war. In the latter, attainment of the resonance condition causes a deflection of the molecules in the beam, detected by change in the particle flux reaching the detection screen.

The most evident advantages of the new methods can be summed up in two words : simplicity and generality. One has only to compare the apparatus of atomic beams, with its ultra high vacuum pumps, its oven, diaphragms, focussing fields of complex geometry and its detectors, with the equipment for magnetic resonance described above to be able to appreciate the gain in simplicity. In particular, each new molecule poses a new problem for generating a molecular beam and also for detection, whereas the radiofrequency methods are applicable to a sample in any state, liquid or solid, amorphous or crystalline, conductor or insulator, provided it can be placed inside the detection coil.

There is of course the other side of the coin. In a molecular beam experiment, a molecule with a nuclear spin arriving at the detector liberates several electron volts of energy, and this is the energy which matters as far as the detection is concerned. By contrast, for electromagnetic detection, the energy involved is just that required to flip over the spin, and is of the order of a millionth to a billionth of an electron volt. The result is that the electromagnetic methods are much less sensitive than beam methods. The electromagnetic signals generated by nuclear magnetic resonance are weak signals, and it is no coincidence that discovery of this phenomenon so soon after the war followed a spectacular improvement in radiofrequency technology as part of the war effort. The minimum number of nuclear spins required to give a detectable signal from a given sample by this technique is quite large, of the order of 10^{18} at least. This is not of course prohibitive, since one milligram of water contains 60 times this number of protons. It is no less true that this relatively low sensitivity of the electromagnetic detection scheme makes it necessary to restrict the studies to condensed matter: solids, liquids or in the extreme case, a high pressure gas. In contrast to what happens in beam experiments where the different molecules are practically isolated from each other, in condensed matter the nuclear spins interact with neighbouring spins and with their surroundings. This considerably complicates the properties of the spin system, the resonance lineshapes and the interpretation of the results, but far from being a weakness of nuclear magnetism, is actually its main attraction. As a famous actress once said "If you have a fault you cannot get rid of, turn it into an advantage". This is what nuclear magnetism has done. We shall see just how by examining the applications of the method.

The first and most obvious application is the measurement of the nuclear moments since all that needs to be done is to measure their Larmor frequencies in a known magnetic field. The moments of essentially all the stable isotopes have by now been determined, providing theoreticians interested in nuclear structure with invaluable information about the arrangement of nucleons in the heart of the nucleus.

Conversely, the measurement of the Larmor frequency of a nucleus of known magnetic moment placed in an unknown magnetic field allows us to deduce the intensity of this field. The possibility of measuring and thereby regulating the magnetic field strength rapidly and precisely is an important new result. Before the war, an absolute measurement of field intensity to an accuracy better than one part in ten thousand would have been a major achievement in metrology, only feasible in certain specialized laboratories. Today (1960) thanks to magnetic resonance, it can be accomplished in a few minutes to an accuracy of better than one part in a hundred thousand. An absolute measurement of the earth's magnetic field is a problem all its own, partly because of its interest for geophysics and prospecting, and partly because of its difficulty, since the magnetic resonance signal is approximately proportional to the square of the field intensity and is therefore extremely small in this case. Various laboratories have developed ingenious schemes to circumvent this difficulty and we now have at our disposition magnetometers based on the principle of magnetic resonance which can measure the earth's field with a precision of the order of a part per million.

If the nuclear spins within a sample did not interact, in a perfectly homogeneous magnetic field they would all have exactly the same Larmor frequency and the resonance line would be infinitely narrow. In reality they are coupled together by magnetic interactions and it is useful (if not entirely correct) to describe these in terms of the concept of a local field. A given spin "sees" not only the applied field, but also the local fields generated by its neighbours superimposed on the main field. This local field varies from one spin to the next and so does the total field "seen" by each spin. The result is a distribution of Larmor frequencies within the sample, equivalent to a finite width for the resonance line. This linewidth, and, more generally, the lineshape, depends on the shape of the distribution of local fields, in its turn determined by the relative distances and orientations of the atoms carrying the nuclear spins under investigation. Theory establishes a quite definite relationship between the shape of the observed spectrum and the atomic positions, providing invaluable information about crystal structure which complements that obtained by X-ray studies. For certain problems, such as the determination of the positions of hydrogen atoms, a difficult task by X-ray diffraction, magnetic resonance turns out to be an essential tool.

The ideas outlined above are valid for solid samples where as a general rule the local fields are of the order of one gauss and the relative width of the resonance lines of the order of one part in a thousand or one part in ten thousand. By contrast, the lines from liquids are very much narrower, attaining the extremely small relative widths mentioned earlier. This is the remarkable phenomenon of "motional narrowing". The distances between atoms in liquids are comparable to those in solids and the same is true for the local fields. The new factor is the Brownian motion of the molecules caused by thermal agitation, of which the amplitude and speed are much higher in liquids than in solids. The effect of this motion is to cause the local field to fluctuate at high frequencies, 10^{12} times a second in low-viscosity liquids, a frequency which the nuclear spins are incapable of following. They therefore "see" only the mean value of this fluctuating field, which is much smaller than its instantaneous value; hence the narrowing of the resonance. There too, the theory of random processes applied to Brownian motion provides a quantitative interpretation of these effects.

In a more general way, in between certain solid samples where the local field has its full intensity, and which we are accustomed to call rigid lattices, and liquids of low viscosity where the lines are narrowed by as much as a million times, we can find all the intermediate cases depending on the amplitude and rapidity of the internal motions. Certain solids, such as rubber or alkali metals well below their melting points, exhibit resonance lines that are much narrower than predicted by rigid lattice theory, indicating the presence of internal motions of rotation or diffusion of atoms or molecules. By following the width and shape of the resonance lines as a function of temperature it is possible to monitor these internal motions, detect phase changes and measure activation energies.

Another important parameter which provides valuable information on internal motion within the sample is what is known as the spin-lattice relaxation time. When a sample is placed in a magnetic field there is a partial orientation of the nuclear moments parallel to the field, but this does not occur instantaneously. We know that once this orientation has been established, the nuclear polarization, that is to say the excess of parallel spins over antiparallel spins (for spin $1/2$ nuclei), must be a function of the temperature, and under conditions where the Curie law applies, must be inversely proportional to the absolute temperature. There must therefore be some mechanism which couples thermal motions to the nuclear moments, in effect "informing" the latter about the temperature of their environment, allowing them to take up suitable orientations according to the laws of thermodynamics. This mechanism is called spin-lattice relaxation and the time constant for the establishment of thermal equilibrium has received the name spin-lattice relaxation time, represented in the literature by the symbol T_1. Here lattice is taken to mean all the degrees of freedom of the sample except nuclear spins; it is a generalization from the first experiments which were concerned only with vibrations in a crystalline lattice.

In the last fifteen years there have been innumerable determinations of relaxation times in liquids and solids. Depending on the chemical nature of the sample, its physical state, its temperature, its purity, and the nuclear species under investigation, the relaxation time may vary between a small fraction of a second and values as long as a minute, an hour, a day or even longer. In certain cases the relaxation time is only limited by our ability to eliminate spurious relaxation mechanisms caused by impurities.

Here too, a detailed theory has explained the observed relaxation times qualitatively and sometimes quantitatively, and perhaps rather better than lineshape studies, relaxation measurements have become an invaluable instrument for investigating what we might call microscopic motion in condensed matter. Among the most recent efforts in this field, one that stands out is the study of the isotopic species ^{3}He, either pure or in solution in ^{4}He, which turns out to be one of the most sophisticated methods for investigating the so-called quantum liquids.

So far we have neglected the effects of coupling between the nuclei and the electron cloud of atoms and molecules. This coupling has different implications and different consequences depending on whether the substances under consideration possess electron magnetism.

In substances without electron magnetism, which are in fact the vast majority, the effect of the electrons on the nuclear resonance condition shows itself first of all by what is called the diamagnetic shielding or chemical shift of the resonance frequency. Under the influence of an applied magnetic field, the electron shells become polarized and induce a weak magnetic field at the position of the nucleus which is superimposed on the external field and causes a small displacement of the nuclear Larmor frequency. This shift naturally depends on the electronic environment of the nucleus, and for identical nuclei situated in different molecules, or in different sites in the same molecule, it results in a fine structure in the spectrum. It is in this way that ethyl alcohol, to cite a famous example, gives a proton magnetic resonance spectrum containing three adjacent resonance lines of relative intensity 1:2:3, corresponding to the hydroxyl, methylene and methyl groups respectively. The structure is in fact rendered even more complex by what are known as the indirect nuclear spin-spin interactions, distinguishable from the usual dipolar couplings that are responsible for the local fields described above. These indirect couplings arise as follows. The weak field generated by a nuclear moment polarizes the electron cloud which in its turn induces a magnetic field at the site of a second neighbouring nuclear moment, of intensity proportional to the moment of the first nucleus. This coupling between the induced field and the second nucleus shows up as an interaction between the two nuclear spins, superimposed on the direct dipolar interaction, and having the remarkable property of not being averaged to zero by the Brownian motion in a liquid, thus contributing to the fine structure of the spectrum.

If I seem to have spent some time over these extremely small effects, it is because this type of study of complex spectra, known as the high resolution method, has taken on in recent years an extraordinary importance for chemistry. The number, positions and intensities of the different lines in the spectrum provide rich and detailed information about molecular structure. The changes in the spectrum as a function of solvent, temperature, and various catalysts, yield chemical reaction rates and help understand the reaction mechanism. It is a fair estimate that more than half the resonance instruments and more than half of the publications on nuclear magnetic resonance are devoted to chemical studies based on high resolution methods, and it happens that at scientific meetings the magnetic resonance physicists feel somewhat overwhelmed by the drive and enthusiasm of their chemist colleagues. Without wishing to go as far as a great physicist who once said, "When the chemists decide to enter a field, it's time to get out", it is important to keep a sense of proportion and admit that high resolution, interesting though it may be, is still only a limited field within the whole of nuclear magnetism.

With regard to substances which possess electron magnetism, interactions between nuclear spins and electron spins sometimes take on aspects of a family quarrel; does their study belong in the field of nuclear magnetism or electron magnetism? It must be said that electron magnetism, while being much more amenable to static magnetic susceptibility measurements than nuclear magnetism, has nevertheless benefitted enormously from the methods of resonance, first applied in this field by the Russian scientist Zavoisky in 1944. This was a major discovery. In this technique, the interaction between electron and nuclear moments shows up as a multiplet structure on the electron resonance line, known as the hyperfine structure. It may be simply explained by saying that the magnetic field generated by the nucleus and "seen" by the electron adopts different values depending on the discreet orientations allowed for the nuclear moment; hence there are different values for the total field experienced by the electron, hence different values of the electron Larmor frequency and thus several spectral lines. It may be recalled that it was the observation of hyperfine structure in optical spectra which led Pauli, as long ago as 1924, to propose the existence of nuclear magnetic moments. Such disputes are Byzantine; nothing relating to the magnetic properties of the nucleus should be excluded from the study of nuclear magnetism. The many aspects of electron-nucleus interaction within magnetic materials are so varied in nature that it is scarcely possible to enumerate all of them in this lecture. Depending on the nature of the substance, metal, semiconductor, insulator, depending on its physical state, liquid or solid, depending on the character of the electron magnetism, paramagnetism, ferromagnetism or antiferromagnetism, according to temperature, and finally the magnetic dilution of the electron moments, the nuclear resonance spectrum may run the whole gamut from complete disappearance of the signal to only a very slight shift of the Larmor frequency.

We mention as an example two kinds of information that may be extracted from such studies. First, the shape of the electron wavefunction, and more specifically its value at the site of the nuclear moment, which thus behaves as a microscopic probe capable of measuring the electron density without perturbing it in any way. In certain substances such as silicon it has been possible in this way to draw up a veritable map of the electron charge distribution. Another instance might be the investigation of the density of states in the case where these electronic states form a continuous spectrum, as in a metal. A recent example that can be quoted is a beautiful confirmation of the new theories of superconductivity by measuring the relaxation time of aluminium in its superconducting state. The temperature dependence of this relaxation time in the neighbourhood of the transition temperature has confirmed the existence of a discontinuity in the distribution of electronic states, as predicted by the theory.

Spin and magnetic moment are not the only properties of the nucleus which play a role in nuclear magnetism. Another is the electric quadrupole moment, a measure of the distortion of the nuclear charge distribution from spherical symmetry. The quadrupole moment is zero for perfect spherical symmetry, positive for an elongated shape similar to that of a cigar and negative for a flattened distribution such as that of a tangerine. In the highly inhomogeneous electrostatic fields found inside a sample of matter there are different discreet orientations available to a quadrupolar nucleus, and a radiofrequency field may interact with the nuclear magnetic moment to induce transitions between these various energy states. In the same way that the coupling of a nuclear moment with an electron moment provides information about electron density at the site of the nucleus, so the coupling of quadrupole moments with electrostatic field gradients provides information about electron distribution inside the material.

These few examples serve to show how, although resonance detection necessitates the use of sample in condensed phases, this is less of a restriction than might be expected since it has been found to be a rich source of new information, which we have in no way exhausted so far.

I would now like to turn to another aspect of nuclear magnetism which I find particularly attractive and which is not always given sufficient emphasis: its role as a model quantum-mechanical system.

An isolated spin I in a magnetic field with its $(2I + 1)$ energy states is one of the simplest quantum systems imaginable, infinitely more simple than the hydrogen atom. The properties of a large assembly of such spins, with mutual interactions and coupling to the environment (the lattice), although incomparably more complex than that of an isolated spin, nervertheless provide problems for the theoretician in statistical mechanics or non-equilibrium thermodynamics which may be rigourously formulated if not always solved completely. These problems are simple enough for at least an approximate solution, or, better still, lead to theoretical predictions that are rigorous although incomplete. They are nevertheless of sufficient complexity that they throw light on the behaviour of other physical systems that are much more complicated. One could object that this is nothing new and that physicists from time immemorial have dreamed up simplified models for the problems they were working on. With their characteristic taste for practical matters, English physicists have often been led to construct mechanical models with a multiplicity of springs, rods and diaphragms.

With nuclear spins we have the advantage of being able to use as models the real systems generously provided by nature where we can write down an exact expression for all the interactions (the Hamiltonian) and even more important, where theoretical predictions or working hypotheses may be verified by means of simple precise experiments. I remember reading in my youth a book by the English author Aldous Huxley, *Beyond the Mexique Bay*. His suggestions might seem a little childish to my learned economist, sociologist and anthropologist colleagues, but they impressed me at the time. Huxley maintained that the tiny republics of Central America, living in relative isolation from the rest of the world if not from one another, constitute a simplified model that provides insight into the behaviour of the much more complex European powers. His principal message was that the root cause of war could not reside in economic factors since these small States were continually at war although he could find no economic reasons for these conflicts.

It matters very little whether he was correct or not. I believe that nuclear spins resemble these republics in that they provide scale models of more highly developed and complex societies, such as that of the electrons in a metal or the atoms in a sample of liquid helium.

The concept of spin temperature, which has proved a fertile source of information on the collective properties of nuclear spins, serves as an example of the point made above. Statistical mechanics states that when a system S is weakly coupled to a second very large system called the thermal reservoir, then S is not in a well-defined energy state but rather has a certain probability of being found in any one of its energy states E_n. This probalility has the value $\exp(-E_n/kT)$ which is smaller the higher the value of E_n. This is the famous Boltzmann law, where k is the Boltzmann constant and T is the absolute temperature of the reservoir. If the system S is large enough, that is if it has sufficient degrees of freedom, and if it also satisfies certain other conditions such as ergodicity, it can become a reservoir itself and we can assign it a temperature even if it is completely isolated.

As we saw earlier, certain substances have extremely long spin-lattice relaxation times and it is possible to accept that the nuclear spins, though coupled together, are completely isolated from the outside world for periods sufficiently long that their behaviour can be properly studied. Even though the spin-spin interactions are well characterized and the problem consequently well defined, it is difficult to prove from first principles that an internal statistical equilibrium is established that can be represented by a temperature. In fact certain physicists of stature were inclined to doubt it. On the other hand, if as a working hypothesis we *assume* the rapid establishment of such a thermal equilibrium, it is possible to conceive and carry out experiments to test this hypothesis. In this way it has been possible to show that under suitable precisely defined conditions the spin system rapidly attains (in a time T_2 much shorter than the spin-lattice relaxation time T_1) an internal thermal equilibrium described by a spin temperature that has all the properties of a thermodynamic temperature, and which can be quite different from that of the rest of the sample.

This state of affairs has the curious consequence that it is possible to define negative temperatures and also achieve them in practice. According to the Boltzmann formula a negative temperature corresponds to higher occupation numbers for the higher energy states. For the vast majority of physical systems, in particular for all systems with motional degrees of freedom, such a concept is absurd, for it would require that the mean energy of the system be infinite. This is not the case for our well-isolated societies of nuclear spins where the form of the Hamiltonian is such that there is a finite upper limit to their total energy, and there is nothing in principle against the idea of a negative temperature, that is to say that the highest energy states could have the highest populations. It has been possible to prepare spin systems in such states and to verify that a self-consistent thermodynamic scheme can be constructed which does not exclude the existence of negative temperatures; this can be demonstrated by true calorimetric experiments which bring two spin systems into thermal contact, one with a positive temperature and one with a negative temperature.

We may remark in passing that contrary to what we might be tempted to think, a negative temperature is *warmer* in the sense of Carnot's Principle than any positive temperature. Essentially, a system at a negative temperature, with the high energy states having the highest populations, has *too much* energy and will give this up if placed in contact with a system at a positive temperature.

On a similar topic we can say that thanks to nuclear spin we can now join the race towards very low temperatures and take a further step towards absolute zero. Today (1960) it is possible to obtain temperatures between 4K and 1K routinely in the laboratory using the common isotope ^{4}He, reaching 0.3K with the rare isotope ^{3}He, and via adiabatic demagnetization much lower temperatures still, down to a thousandth of a degree Kelvin.

Can one go still lower? In order to answer this question in the affirmative and at the same time provide a physical rationale for the experiment, it is necessary to find systems that possess properties which continue to have an observable temperature dependence below 0.001 K. Now, at such temperatures matter is frozen into a state of almost perfect order. As the temperature is reduced step by step the implacable Boltzmann law returns each physical system, one after the other, into its ground state. The crystal vibrations are the first to obey, the electron moments of paramagnetic materials the last, but at 0.001 K they are all frozen into an order which may then only change imperceptibly. Everything that is, except the nuclear spins, which due to the weakness of their interactions only achieve an ordered state at temperatures below a microkelvin. Such temperatures have not yet been attained (in 1960) but there is every reason to hope that they will be and that we may then observe strange new phenomena like nuclear ferromagnetism and antiferromagnetism.

If we wished to classify physical phenomena according to the order of magnitude of their characteristic energies, it would be natural to place atomic and molecular physics in the centre of this scale. There we find the excitation and ionization energies of the valence electrons, bond energies of molecules, cohesive energies of solids, all of the order of magnitude of one electron volt. At one extreme of the scale there is nuclear physics with its energies measured in millions of electron volts, and then meson and hyperon physics involving billions and tens of billions of electron volts. At the other extreme, right at the bottom of the scale, there are the energies associated with nuclear magnetism, measured in millionths or billionths of an electron volt.

Nevertheless the two extremes come together at more than one point. I have already made mention of the measurement of nuclear magnetic moments, to which may be added quadrupole moments, which provide valuable information about nuclear structure. But there is more. When a nuclear reaction takes place, it is quite certain that the magnetic forces which come into play between the magnetic moments of the two colliding particles are entirely negligible with respect to the nuclear forces. However these nuclear forces depend on the relative orientations of the spins of the two particles, spins that are parallel to the magnetic moments. The nuclear moment provides a "handle" that carries the nuclear spin with it. We can thus appreciate how it is that infinitesimally weak interactions can have an influence on phenomena involving enormously higher energies. In nuclear reactions, as in radioactive decay, the nuclear spins are oriented at random and the observable parameters represent mean values averaged over all possible orientations. This loss of information is regrettable and there would be considerable interest in an experiment which oriented the nuclear spins not only of the radioactive nuclei but also of the stable nuclei that are used as targets for nuclear reactions. In the case of radioactive nuclei, some remarkable results have already been obtained. My colleague Leprince-Ringuet has pointed out how some long and patient measurements of very high precision by high energy physicists showed that the half-lives of θ and τ mesons were the same, leading the theoreticians Lee and Yang to the concept of non-conservation of parity. I would like to jump on this bandwagon by reminding you that the crucial experiment which brilliantly established the principle of non-conservation was the observation of the anisotropy of the β emission from ^{60}Co nuclei oriented at low temperature. It was only possible to obtain and study this orientation thanks to a thorough understanding of the hyperfine interactions of the nuclear magnetic moments with the electron clouds, the result of long and patient theoretical and experimental studies of magnetic resonance.

In the case of radioactive nuclei the polarization of an infinitesimal proportion of the nuclei in the sample is sufficient for the experiment. It is a much more difficult problem to prepare polarized targets where *all* the nuclear spins of the sample (or at least a sizable proportion) are polarized. Appreciable progress on polarized targets was achieved by the methods of dynamic polarization. These require a profound understanding of the interactions between nuclear spins and electron spins and their relaxation mechanisms. They can boost the nuclear polarization by factors of several hundred. With suitable samples we have managed to achieve proton polarizations of the order of 20 % in our laboratory, that is to say 200 times more intense than the natural polarization under the same conditions of temperature and magnetic field (1960). Such polarizations are sufficient for the purpose of observing the nuclear effects. What remains is the tricky problem of making these targets "operational" in the sense of directing a beam of particles from an accelerator onto the target sample buried inside a metal cavity, plunged into liquid helium, enclosed in a Dewar vessel and finally placed between the poles of an electromagnet.

This is the kind of restriction which some of our nuclear physics colleagues do not always fully appreciate. Attracted by polarized targets, but reluctant to make more effort in the experiment than with an ordinary target, they remind one of that hard-to-please spectator at the circus who, seeing an acrobat riding a bicycle on a tightrope high above the ring with a lighted lantern on his head while playing Kreuzer's sonata, pours scorn on the performance saying "I have heard it played much better by Menuhin".

If I were to try to put in a nutshell the essential character of nuclear magnetism I would be tempted to say that it is a discipline on a human scale, in more than one sense. More and more, the growing complexity of both experimental and theoretical techniques has forced the physicists into an excessive specialization where an expert on muons tends to neglect K mesons, or a rare earth chemist neglects the alkali metals. Nuclear magnetism has contacts with quite diverse disciplines such as quantum mechanics, statistical mechanics, the theory of random processes, atomic and molecular structure, classical magnetism, the vast field of solid state physics and finally nuclear physics, and thereby serves to re-establish in physics the true generalist with an appreciation of all the fields.

On the experimental front I have already mentioned the demanding requirements imposed on the equipment, with electromagnets weighing two or three tons and high-technology radiofrequency circuitry. Nevertheless we are still a long way from the monsters used by nuclear physics and high energy physics and it is still possible to work alone on a project without having to mobilize an army of engineers and technicians. Finally the theory is not so difficult as to make it impossible for a physicist to explain what he has observed and also make predictions about the nature and magnitude of the new phenomena he proposes to observe. There is much talk of the exaltation of the great scientists as they seize the opportunity of a new unexpected discovery. What of the joy and astonishment when a new phenomenon anticipated by the theory shows up as predicted and exactly where it was expected?

It is true of course that in nuclear magnetism we only scratch the surface of things. The important problem—the real problem—is to understand what lies beneath, that is to say the nature of elementary particles and their interactions. The importance of this challenge fully justifies the immense efforts invested in it. My colleague Leprince-Ringuet has spoken of the anxiety, not to say anguish, which he felt when confronted by the enormous and inhuman scale of the equipment used for high energy physics, and the collectively-owned, industrial-scale giant machines. And what of the theory? Well in that field there are vacancies for a rather special kind of manpower, a genius or two. From time to time one appears, makes some kind of break-through, while the rest stumble around and beat their heads against the many brick walls. Unfortunately the break-throughs are very rare and the unproductive periods very long.

So many young theorists, intelligent and hardworking though they are, wear themselves out in unproductive efforts trying to sprinkle a little salt on the tail of the Almighty (Huxley again), that I wonder whether they should not be dissuaded from this career at an earlier stage. Perhaps CERN, which from time to time advertises in the newspapers, openings in an exciting, tax-free career should face up to this problem and ask for "genius without special experience, no one older than 25 need apply." When all is said and done, I am happy to be working in a field where, with hard work and a modicum of talent, one can hope to make a useful contribution.

Nuclear Magnetism

II. THE DAWN OF 1984: MAGNUS

Some new concepts. Instrumental advances: high fields, low temperatures, electronics, computers. High resolution in liquids. High resolution in solids. Magnetic resonance imaging. Superfluid helium-3. Polarized targets. Pseudomagnetism. Nuclear magnetic ordering.

On one point at least, George Orwell, with his terrifying vision of *1984*, made no mistake: the canker of abbreviations and acronyms is eating away at our language. Nuclear magnetism may not yet have taken on the Orwellian abbreviation "Magnuc"* but for a long time now nuclear magnetic resonance has been universally called NMR, no doubt because the former is a science, the latter a much more commonplace technique. Let us compromise and call our new character "Magnus" which is just as short but less horrible. It will be Magnus from now on.

In the previous chapter Magnus was fifteen years old; here he is in his forties. From Cherubin to Bartholo, or nearly. In fact the analogy is false at both extremes. At fifteen years old, Magnus is not the wild indecisive Cherubin. He is a strong healthy fellow with well-established ideas and ways; and although his development has sometimes advanced by leaps and bounds, there was never any need for an agonising reappraisal of the

---

* Short for the French *magnétisme nucléaire*.

picture he presented at fifteen. Nor is he today the disillusioned old fogey Bartholo, but a vigourous forty-year-old with a promising future. The purpose of this short article is to sketch with a broad brush what has happened to the Magnus of 1960 at the beginning of 1984. My story will necessarily be incomplete and probably biased; the emphasis placed on such-and-such project depends on the tastes and interests of the friend of Magnus who is telling the story. I shall try not to overemphasize the fields in which I have been most involved; as credible as a drunkard's pledge, some would say.

In order to understand the new period in Magnus' life it is necessary to recall the methods and concepts that were known long before his fifteenth year, but not mentioned in the chapter, "The Early Years". It might have been possible to ignore these ideas when hobnobbing with the young Magnus, but they are indispensible for those who are interested in his mature years. These are pulse methods, free precession, the rotating frame, adiabatic passage and adiabatic demagnetization. In the first chapter we described magnetic resonance as a forced precession of the nuclear magnetization about the applied magnetic field, caused by the action of a weak radiofrequency field tuned to the Larmor frequency. If this excitation field is rapidly shut off, precession will persist for a short while before decaying to zero. This is called free precession. In order to excite this free precession there is no need to wait for the nuclear magnetization to reach some steady-state condition, all that is required is a short intense pulse of the radiofrequency field at resonance. This is what is known as a pulse method. It is a general method for all resonant systems whatever their physical nature. There is a mathematical relation between the frequency-domain response and the impulse response of all such systems. In the case of nuclear spins the former is the response to a weak, continuous excitation swept slowly through the resonance condition (the "slow-passage" method) while the latter is the decaying time-domain signal following a short pulse (the "free induction decay"). This mathematical relationship, which operates in both the forward and reverse senses, is Fourier transformation. The information content of an NMR spectrum obtained by slow passage is thus equivalent to that obtained by the pulse method provided that the pulse is sufficiently intense to excite all the spectral components simultaneously, for example the ethanol spectrum described in Chapter 1. We shall see the consequences of this later.

The concept of the rotating frame of reference is a special case of a quite general method for describing a given motion in its simplest form by choosing a particular coordinate system. It is well-known that such a change of reference frame may entail the addition of certain inertial forces, such as the Coriolis force, to the forces already acting on the system. In magnetic resonance the spins are excited by a weak radiofrequency field orthogonal to the applied field at a frequency ω close to the Larmor frequency ω_0. Generally this is a linearly polarizd field, equivalent to the superposition of two equal counterrotating fields, and the component which rotates in the opposite sense to the Larmor precession has negligible effect and can be safely neglected. Only the component which rotates in the right sense need therefore be considered, a field H_I rotating at an angular frequency ω close to ω_0 around the applied field H_0 wich is very much larger than H_I. In a frame rotating in synchronism with H_I the latter apperars as a static transverse field, a considerable simplification. Transformation to the rotating frame involves replacing the applied field H_0 with a fictitious field ΔH proportional to the resonance offset $(\omega - \omega_0)$ which of course goes to zero at exact resonance. To adopt an anthropomorphic picture, we may say that in the rotating frame the spins "see" only a single "effective field" that is the resultant of the longitudinal field ΔH and the transverse field H_I. The motion of the spins in this frame is a Larmor precession about the effective field and only a very simple transformation is required to convert this motion to a laboratory-based coordinate frame. If the radiofrequency field H_I is applied far from resonance, ΔH is much larger than H_I and the effective field is essentially parallel to the applied field H_0 and hence to the equilibrium magnetization M_0. When ω approaches ω_0, ΔH decreases and the effective field makes a larger and larger angle with respect to H_0 so that at exact resonance it becomes identical to H_I. Continuation of the sweep beyond the resonance condition turns the effective field even further from the direction of H_0 so that it eventually ends up antiparallel to it. Provided that the process is sufficiently slow ("adiabatic") the nuclear magnetization that was initially aligned along the effective field (the only field it "sees" in this frame) is said to "follow" the effective field, remaining always parallel to it as the sweep passes through resonance. This is known as adiabatic passage. Thus at exact resonance the nuclear magnetization is at right angles to the applied field, while on the far side of resonance it is antiparallel to it.

Another operation that can be carried out on the nuclear spins is called "adiabatic demagnetization in the rotating frame". In order to understand this experiment it is first necessary to recall the more common "adiabatic demagnetization" technique, which we should now distinguish by the name "demagnetization in the laboratory frame". This involves a progressive reduction in magnetic field intensity H_o carried out sufficiently slowly that there is no increase in the state of disorder of the spin system characterised by a quantity the thermodynamicists call entropy. In such an operation, said to be "adiabatic", where the magnetic energy of the spin system decreases in absolute terms while the entropy stays constant, thermodynamics tells us that the absolute temperature of the system falls, often by a considerable amount. In the case of electron spins which have an appreciable heat capacity and which are strongly coupled to their environment (the lattice), this constitutes a very effective method of cooling the sample, a discovery made over half a century ago by Giauque and Debye which earned them a Nobel prize. By contrast, nuclear spins, as we saw in Chapter 1, may remain isolated from the rest of the sample for long periods owing to their long spin-lattice relaxation times. Adiabatic demagnetization of a nuclear spin system lowers only the spin temperature which can reach a value that is orders of magnitude lower than the initial temperature. This cooling effect is expressed as the ratio T_i/T_f where T_i is the initial temperature and T_f the final temperature; this ratio is of the order of H_o/H_L where H_o is the strong applied field and H_L is the local field at the nucleus.

Let us return to the subject of the rotating frame. At exact resonance, when the longitudinal field ΔH has been progressively reduced to zero, the nuclear spins see only the weak field H_1 which appears to be a static field in this frame. We may then take the last step which is to suppress the radiofrequency field H_1 and thereby cool the nuclear spins as effectively as by the standard adiabatic demagnetization experiment without altering the strong applied field H_0. There is a further twist to the story. Depending on the sense of the resonance offset $(\omega-\omega_0)$ the initial condition of the effective field is either parallel to H_0 and to the nuclear magnetization, as tacitly assumed above, or antiparallel. In the latter case the nuclear spins are at a negative temperature (as defined in Chapter 1) in the rotating frame, and remain so until the final demagnetization step. We shall see later how this fact can be put to good use.

After this rather dry but indispensable description of concepts already well established by the year 1960, let us return to the story of Magnus and his career. Fundamental to his progress are the technological advances made in the last 25 years. Some allow things to be done better than before while others make experiments feasible that previously seemed impossible or even unthinkable. These developments fall into four separate categories.

First, there has been a considerable increase in available magnetic field intensity and in its stability. This progress stems from the use of superconducting materials of the "second kind" which are capable of supporting very intense fields without losing their superconductivity. Fundamental research has provided an understanding of the nature of superconductivity while technological research has perfected the methods of fabrication. It used to be that a field of 2 to 3 tesla was the practical limit for the iron magnets used in the laboratory, but now we may go to 6, then 8, then 10, and even to 12 tesla using superconducting solenoids, with homogeneities comparable to the best iron magnets and much better stabilities.

Secondly, there has been a significant lowering of the temperatures available in the laboratory. Originally the limit had been 0.8 K obtained by evaporation of helium-4 under vigourous pumping, then 0.25 K by pumping on the rare isotope helium-3, and then a progressive reduction towards 100, then 50, then 20 millikelvin or lower through the use of the new dilution refrigerators. In these devices a certain quantity of helium-3 is dissolved in helium-4, greatly increasing the entropy of the mixture with respect to that of the separate constituents. The consequent reduction in the temperature may be understood by analogy with the cooling which occurs when a liquid evaporates. We all remember the sensation of cold created when a drop of a volatile liquid like ether falls on the skin. The process of dissolving atoms of helium-3 in helium-4 is equivalent to their evaporation in the previous type of refrigerator. The figure of 20 millikelvin mentioned above is the value obtained *routinely* in many laboratories. In those which specialize in the low-temperature research described below, dilution refrigeration is used to reach one millikelvin or even below. It is often convenient to use the reciprocal temperature $(1/T)$ for which we have invented the unit nivlek (kelvin spelt backwards) which means that one millikelvin is equivalent to one kilonivlek. To tell the truth, this ingenious definition has not been widely adopted outside our laboratory.

Thirdly, there have been the improvements in electronics. Vacuum tubes have of course completely disappeared, replaced by transistors and then by integrated circuits that are much smaller and much more efficient. We have thus witnessed spectacular progress in the range of methods available for exciting nuclear spins and for processing the detected signals.

Finally, the last and perhaps most important advance on the practical level has been achieved by computers and data processing. This has been inextricably bound up with the development of integrated circuitry mentioned above, but remains distinct in the way it is utilized.

High resolution spectroscopy of liquids, which was already one of the prize activities of Magnus in the early years, has nothing to benefit from low-temperature technology but has exploited some other advances up to the hilt. Increased field stability has been an obvious boon. But it is the increased field intensity that has had the greatest impact. This leads to an enhancement of signal strength, partly due to the increased equilibrium magnetization M_0 and partly due to the increase in the electromotive force induced in the coil by the precessing nuclear magnetization, also proportional to the Larmor frequency. Each of these parameters M_0 and ω_0 is effectively proportional to the magnetic field intensity. There is another more subtle effect. We saw in Chapter 1 that high resolution spectra are rich in information since they include the effects of both chemical shift and spin-spin coupling. This becomes an embarassment of riches for cases where the chemical shifts and coupling constants are of the same order of magnitude, for then the number of allowed transitions becomes very large. The individual signals are then weaker and above all the interpretation becomes very difficult. High applied fields increase the chemical shifts at the expense of the coupling constants which are field-independent, thus simplifying the spectra enormously. Also, by concentrating the intensity of the spectrum into fewer lines, the intensities of the latter are strongly enhanced.

Advances in data processing have achieved an even more radical transformation of high resolution spectroscopy. Recording such a spectrum by the slow passage method is inconvenient and tedious, limiting the through-put of spectra and imposing severe demands on stability. Pulse excitation followed by observation of the free precession signal provides the same information as the slow passage spectrum but requires a much shorter time, provided that the decoding operation (Fourier transformation) can be carried out quickly. Modern computers can implement this last step in "real time", that is to say during the NMR experiment. This speeding up of the process of gathering information allows many different spectra to be recorded in a short time, or permits sensitivity enhancement by accumulating the same spectrum a large number of times in the computer memory. One of the most important consequences has been the possibility of studying carbon-13 spectra of organic compounds despite the low natural abundance (1 %) and the low magnetogyric ratio, one quarter that of the proton. Another recent refinement of high resolution spectroscopy attributable to the advances in data processing methods is two-dimensional Fourier transformation; we shall try to explain the end-result, if not the implementation, by an analogy.

In a high resolution spectrum there is no simple correlation between the positions of the various lines in the spectrum and the sites of the nuclear spins within the molecule, or the mutual interactions between these spins.

One could imagine an analogy with a group photograph, where the members of various different families are thrown together at random so that it is impossible to trace the family connections. If it were possible to order, "Smiths, one step forward, Jones family, two steps forward, Robinsons, one pace to the rear, etc." and then take separate photographs of each row where there is now only a single family, the identification process would be greatly simplified. In a similar way it is possible to take a complicated spectrum full of overlapping lines and decompose it into a series of well-separated subspectra where membership of a given subspectrum would have a real structural significance.

Towards the end of the nineteen sixties, Magnus found another area of activity which has since grown spectacularly, that is high resolution in the solid state. This might come as a surprise to the reader who learned in Chapter 1 that resonance lines in solids are severely broadened by local magnetic fields (which by convention we shall now call dipolar fields) to the extent that all fine structure due to chemical shifts and indirect spin-spin coupling was completely masked. This should be constrasted with the case of liquids where rapid molecular motion averages the dipolar interactions to zero and thus permits high resolution studies.

An idea which saw the light of day at the end of the nineteen fifties was that this absence of internal motion in the solid state might be countered by imposing a rapid macroscopic rotation of the sample with respect to the magnetic field direction, using a small turbine. One can show that if the motion is sufficiently fast, to be precise, faster than the Larmor precession frequency would be in a field equal to the local dipolar field, the latter field appears to be considerably reduced as far as the nuclear spins are concerned. A second requirement is that the rotation axis should be inclined at the "magic angle" with respect to the direction of the applied magnetic field; the magic angle is one half of the tetrahedral angle, or the angle between a body diagonal of a cube and one of its edges. Although interesting results have been obtained by this method in certain cases, the required rotation speeds are often prohibitive. It was therefore quite natural to think of replacing macroscopic rotation of the sample by a forced rotation of the spins themselves at the magic angle, a rotation brought about by suitable intense radiofrequency fields. An important step forward was to implement this idea not with a continuous radiofrequency field but by a suitably designed sequence of intense radiofrequency pulses, the free precession signal being monitored periodically in a "window" between two adjacent pulses. These methods could be put into practice thanks to the recent progress in electronics, in particular the possibility of using a small computer to control the pulse sequence. The optimization of these pulse sequences for the purposes of reducing the residual dipolar broadening to a minimum and also correcting the errors due to pulse imperfections, has led to some interesting mathematical developments. High resolution in the solid state is a striking example of a situation where a new idea has emerged at just the right moment to be able to exploit a new technology.

Note that when it comes to the results, high resolution in the solid state provides *more* than just the observation of spectra of samples which cannot be converted into the liquid state. As explained in Chapter 1, chemical shifts and indirect spin-spin coupling, unlike dipolar coupling, are not averaged to zero by the Brownian motion of liquids. Nevertheless an appreciable part of this information, such as the anisotropy with respect to the molecular axes, is lost by this averaging process. This is the information that high resolution in the solid state can recover.

Now although Magnus is naturally a very discreet person, a metamorphosis occurred recently which placed him in the public eye and on the lips of government ministers. This is an extremely important technique which has made enormous progress since 1975 and which promises eventually to provide diagnostic medicine and clinical research with a tool that surpasses X-ray tomography. One of the pioneers has called this "Zeugmatography" but fortunately the term does not seem to have caught on; today the method is normally referred to as NMR imaging. While the basic principle of the method is very simple, its implementation is complicated and owes more to computer science than to physics, as in fact does X-ray tomography. We shall therefore limit the discussion to some very simple ideas.

Just as X-ray imaging measures the electron density, NMR imaging measures the density of protons, which is high throughout the human body. The key to the NMR method is to be able to correlate the proton signal with the spatial coordinates, perhaps as a function of time. Many different methods have been proposed and used for this purpose. The basic idea is to superimpose a magnetic field gradient on the applied static field; this can be achieved by supplying currents (that may be programmed to vary with time) to auxiliary coils surrounding the sample. For example, a linear gradient suitably modulated makes it possible to limit the observed signal to a plane normal to the gradient. Superposition of two such gradients at right angles restricts the signal to a line, and if three gradients are used, to a point, the so-called "hot spot".

In actual practice the more recent machines save time by a more complicated form of correlation between the signal and the spatial coordinates. At each instant a computer program controls the currents in the various auxiliary coils and the intensity of the radiofrequency pulses which excite the spins, storing the corresponding array of free precession signals in memory. A complex computer algorithm is used to reconstruct the image, that is to say the spatial distribution of the protons.

As with the X-ray method the question of contrast is very important. Two adjacent organs that have sufficiently distinct proton densities, for example bone and the surrounding muscle, show up on the final image in high contrast. Alternatively one can make use of differences in the values of the spin-lattice relaxation time T_1 which has an influence on the strength of the signal and which may vary from one organ to another. It has been found that the protons in cancerous cells have a longer T_1 than in normal cells and this may be used to detect such tumours. The other relaxation time T_2 which measures the rate of decay of transverse nuclear magnetization, also exhibits useful variations between different organs.

Magnetic resonance of nuclei other than protons has also been shown to have medical applications. The most interesting of these is phosphorus-31 which shows quite large chemical shifts for different molecules, allowing us to follow some important biochemical reactions between these molecules. The dream would be to use phosphorus resonances for imaging. Unfortunately the abundance of phosphorus in the living organism (calculated for the ensemble, rather than a specific organ rich in this element) and the lower nuclear moment both conspire to make this method about a thousandfold less sensitive than the proton method, which is scarcely encouraging.

In order to construct a magnet large enough to accept the whole body of a patient, one can use either an air-cored solenoid where the field intensity is limited by the permitted current, or a superconducting solenoid with a capital cost that is much higher but which has lower running costs.

It was in 1972 that the superfluid phases of helium-3 were discovered, and Magnus played an important part in this neat experiment. While it is true that the phase transition was first observed as a feature on the melting curve at the temperature of the order of 2.5 millikelvin, it was only as a result of magnetic resonance measurements that the nature of this transition was understood. It was these experiments which later provided the most complete and detailed description of the nature of superfluid phases.

It is out of the question here to try to give even a brief explanation of the structure of these phases. Let us simply say that they are reasonably similar to that of electrons in a superconductor below the transition temperature where we know that the electrons are associated into pairs, called Cooper pairs, in a condensation process that minimizes their free energy. As far as Magnus is concerned there is one key difference; in superfluid liquid helium-3 the Cooper pairs of spins have the quantum number 1 (rather than zero for the electrons in a superconductor) allowing the observation of magnetic resonance effects that give rise to some surprising properties.

The most important of these, which determines the NMR behaviour, is that the dipolar energy does not go to zero but remains at an appreciable value, in contrast to the case of a normal liquid. This is due to the coherence which exists between different Cooper pairs, described by what is known as the order parameter. There are two superfluid phases, A and B, which at the pressure used to observe the melting curve, appear near 2.6 and 2.2 millikelvin. They have extraordinary magnetic properties. The two phases give rise to magnetic resonance responses, observable in the absence of an applied field, at frequencies Ω_A and Ω_B. The ratio Ω_A^2/Ω_B^2 is 5/2 near the transition temperature.

When an external field is applied the two phases give rise to longitudinal resonances, that is to say responses excited by a radiofrequency field that is parallel to the applied field, and the frequencies Ω_A and Ω_B are the same as those in zero field. One may also observe transverse resonances where the frequency of phase B is equal to the Larmor frequency ω_0 while the frequency of phase A is given by the square root of the sum of the squares of Ω_A and ω_0.

The magnetic resonance of these phases may also by excited by pulses. Their response to such excitation is strange and fascinating, having nothing in common with that of normal liquids, but we shall not describe it here. Suffice it to say that all these properties and many others have been accounted for quantitatively by theory. The discovery of superfluid liquid helium-3 is one of the finest jewels in Magnus' crown.

In the first chapter, I explained why polarized targets are of interest to nuclear physicists and particle physicists, and outlined the difficulties encountered in achieving high polarizations of nuclear spins. I summed up the results obtained at that time and considered what progress remained to be made in the future. These goals have now been achieved. At the end of 1960, polarizations were of the order of 20% in samples measuring a fraction of a cubic centimetre. They were now, at the end of the seventies, very close to 100% (they can scarcely go higher) and exceeded 80% even in samples that have a volume of the order of a *litre*. There is better news still: the nuclear spins that are of interest for particle physics are those of protons; now the polarized targets of 1960 were relatively dilute in polarized protons, only one for every thirty nucleons. This ratio has been improved by a factor five. Finally, as we had always hoped, these targets have been rendered operational, that is to say accessible to the incident particle beams despite the impressive magnetic, cryogenic and electronic hardware that surrounds them.

There are several reasons for these spectacular advances. I have already mentioned the technological progress in superconductivity, cryogenics, and electronics. But there have also been improvements in the sample preparation techniques and in the understanding of the dynamic polarization process that allows us to transfer electron polarizations, which are practically 100%, to the nuclear spins in the same field and at the same temperature.

Having "delivered" his polarized targets to the users who coveted them, Magnus, who was beginning to get bored by the whole business, turned towards another type of polarized target that interested him rather more. It would by the way be more correct to speak of a change in the type of projectile used. The beams of fast protons and mesons with energies measured in millions or billions of electron volts have been replaced by slow neutrons having energies of a small fraction of an electron volt.

It was quite natural for Magnus to be interested in this type of projectile. Slow neutrons are a marvellous tool for the investigation of condensed matter and so is Magnus. They naturally go together. For many years the techniques of slow neutrons and magnetism have been drawn together based on three special properties of neutrons — the absence of charge which allows neutrons to penetrate bulk matter without difficulty, the de Broglie wavelength, comparable to interatomic distances, which allows coherent diffraction from a periodic lattice, and the magnetic moment which can interact with the moments within the sample and thus probe its magnetic properties.

There is one obstacle in the way of this alliance between the neutron and Magnus, and at first sight it appears insurmountable. It is the small size of Magnus. The type of magnetism that has been investigated by neutrons for decades is the magnetism of atoms rather than nuclei, and electron magnetic moments are thousands of times stronger than the weak magnets available to Magnus. Magnetic interactions and therefore scattering amplitudes are thereby reduced by three or four orders of magnitude, while the scattering cross-sections (proportional to the square) are several million times lower. It is the scattering cross-section that determines the observed intensity of the scattered neutron beam. What saves Magnus in the last resort is the existence of a quite different interaction with the neutron, not magnetic in nature but *nuclear*, a coupling of the incident neutron to the target nucleus not through their magnetic moments but through their spins, which are parallel to the moments. The form of this coupling is similar if not identical to that of magnetic interactions but, we repeat, it is not a magnetic force but a *nuclear* force, and for all species of nuclei it is very much larger than the weak magnetic force. For certain nuclei such as the proton it may even be stronger than the magnetic coupling between a neutron and an *electron* moment. In order to compare the magnitudes of these two types of coupling, it is convenient to assign to each nucleus, in addition to its magnetic moment μ a fictitious moment μ^* called the pseudomagnetic moment. It is defined as the magnetic moment that the nucleus would need to possess to give a magnetic interaction between neutron and nucleus equal to the coupling between the spins due to the nuclear force. Defined in this manner, the pseudomagnetic moment of the proton turns out to be five Bohr magnetons, that is to say five times greater than the magnetic moment of the electron. This new manifestation of the interaction between the spins of neutrons and nuclei has come to be called nuclear pseudomagnetism (a term which seems to have caught on rather better than zeumatography or nivlek). Although the neutron-nucleus pseudomagnetic interaction differs in a fundamental way from magnetic interactions, it is nevertheless true that an incident neutron is scattered differently by the two possible proton orientations in a magnetic field, and thereby serves as a probe of Magnus' properties. Any port in a storm.

The concept of nuclear pseudomagnetism is a fertile one and can be taken a step further. It has been known for a long time that in the interior of a magnetized sample, such as a piece of iron or cobalt, the magnetic moment of a neutron is sensitive not to the field H but to the magnetic induction $B = H + 4\pi M$ where M is the macroscopic magnetization. The Larmor frequency of the neutron is thus equal to $\gamma_N B$. The nuclear magnetization $M_n = N\mu P$, where N is the number of nuclei per unit volume, is always very weak even in a target where the polarization P approaches 100%. It is not the same story for nuclear pseudomagnetization $M^*_n = N\mu^* P$ which may have a value of the order of a kilogauss in a strongly polarized proton target. One might hazard a guess (and a rigourous calculation confirms it) that a neutron passing through a polarized nuclear target placed in a magnetic field H would be sensitive to the pseudomagnetic induction $B^* = H + 4\pi M^*$ and have its Larmor precession frequency shifted with respect to its value in a vacuum by a quantity $\gamma_N H^*$, where $H^* = 4\pi M^*$ is a pseudomagnetic field. Experiment completely bears out this hypothesis which had in fact been formulated long before from a different viewpoint by nuclear physicists on quite different considerations. It has even proved possible to carry out a pseudomagnetic resonance experiment where the rotating component of proton magnetization from a polarized target was "perceived" by the incident neutrons as a rotating field that could induce transitions between their spin states. An important application of the concept of pseudomagnetic precession has been the systematic measurement of pseudomagnetic moments of a large number of nuclear species, of which few were previously known. Another application of pseudomagnetism will soon emerge. Despite a long history of startling successes, Magnus has had an inferiority complex because of his small size compared with his big brother, electron magnetism. He lacked the long-range order that his brother had been accustomed to from birth. In the first chapter (1960), I made some allusion to this question on a hopeful note: "Nuclear spins at temperatures below a microkelvin... Such temperatures have not yet been attained but there is every reason to hope that they will be and that we may then observe strange phenomena like nuclear ferromagnetism and antiferromagnetism."

Now they have in fact been observed after years of work, and they are indeed very strange phenomena.

This figure of one microkelvin (or if you wish, a meganivlek) appropriate to the onset of long-range order, is calculated as an order of magnitude in the following way. A nuclear moment μ in a local magnetic field H_L generated by neighbouring nuclei, has an energy μH_L equal to the thermal energy kT_c, where T_c is the transition temperature marking the boundary of the ordered state. We are led to the value of one microkelvin by assuming that the nucleus is a proton and that H_L is about 5 gauss, which is not unreasonable.

In spite of the considerable advances in the technology of cryogenics, described earlier, no existing refrigerator is capable of producing temperatures as low as this, so the only possible method of cooling is adiabatic demagnetization using the nuclear spin system. Consider for example an initial temperature T_i of 10 millikelvin and an initial field of 5 tesla, values that are readily accessible with dilution refrigerators and superconducting solenoids available today. If we assume a local field H_L of 5 gauss, then the final temperature is given by $T_f = T_i(H_L/H_o)$, that is to say one micro-kelvin.

Nevertheless, for historic reasons and also for more fundamental reasons, this "brute force" method is not the one first tried nor the one currently used. The historical rationale is quite simple. When these experiments on nuclear magnetic order were first attempted in the nineteen-sixties the temperature obtainable in a routine fashion was 0.3 K and the magnetic field 2.5 tesla. The former was obtained by one of the early refrigerators using evaporation of helium-3, and the latter by an iron magnet. Under these conditions the final temperature expected by the brute force method would have been about 60 microkelvin, two orders of magnitude too high. Dynamic polarization methods were therefore tried. A 50% polarization of protons in a magnetic field of 2.5 tesla corresponds to an initial spin temperature of 5 millikelvin, and hence to the desired final temperature of the order of a microkelvin after demagnetization.

The adoption of dynamic polarization methods leads to a different formulation of the problem, better adapted to this method. We have earlier mentioned the thermodynamic quantity entropy, which is a function of the temperature of the system and which decreases as the degree of order increases, remaining constant during adiabatic demagnetization. There is a critical temperature T_c at which the ordering of the spin system occurs. This may be associated with a critical value of the entropy $S_c = S(T_c)$. Furthermore, it is possible to show that at high field, the entropy is a decreasing function of the polarization, $S_o(P)$ and depends only on P. If we define a critical polarization P_c according to the equation $S_o(P_c) = S_c$, ordering by demagnetization can occur for any values of initial polarization that are greater than P_c. There is no need to specify the initial values of the field and the spin temperature separately.

Dynamic polarization continues to be used even though the brute force method would seem to be applicable now that better cryogenic methods and intense fields are available; the reasons are quite subtle and will be developed in the arguments which follow.

The secular arm of Magnus, NMR, can only be observed at high field, a fact which appears to be incompatible with the use of NMR to study the final ordered state prepared by adiabatic demagnetization. This is where adiabatic demagnetization in the rotating frame, described earlier (and represented henceforth by the acronym ADRF) can be put to good use. This technique allows the nuclear spin temperature to be sufficiently reduced for ordering to occur while the intense external field is still present, thus permitting NMR detection. This is having one's cake and eating it. One peculiarity of the rotating frame not mentioned when it was first described is the fact that the magnetic dipolar interaction between spins, which is responsible for their low-entropy order, is "perceived" in this frame in a slightly different way than it is perceived in the absence of the external field. Since it is an anisotropic interaction, there are different "effective" dipolar interactions for different orientations of the applied field with respect to the crystal axes. If the sample under investigation is not a single crystal, ADRF produces a nuclear ordering that is a superposition of different arrangements of the spins, appearing at different critical temperatures, in different crystallites. It would not be a "clean" experiment.

If on the other hand the sample is a single crystal, it must be an insulator since the relatively intense radiofrequency fields employed will not penetrate into a metallic sample because of the "skin effect" unless the metal is very finely divided. The sample is thus necessarily a single crystal and an insulator. Unfortunately, in an insulator subjected to fields exceeding one or two tesla at temperatures below 100 millikelvin, the nuclear spin-lattice relaxation time becomes prohibitively long and thermal equilibrium polarizations are *never* reached, precluding the use of the brute force method. This leaves only the dynamic polarization method, which can achieve high polarizations but requires much more modest applied fields and less extreme temperatures than the brute force method, and above all can be completed in a finite time. The logical chain of argument which leads to the adoption of dynamic polarization may be summarized as follows : NMR $\mapsto$ high field $\mapsto$ ADRF $\mapsto$ single crystal $\mapsto$ insulator $\mapsto$ dynamic polarization.

The possibility of studying nuclear magnetic ordering by NMR is not the only advantage of ADRF. An investigation of the effects of orientation in the applied magnetic field brings to light a host of new structures in contrast to the single structure obtained by classic demagnetization. A rich new field of study arises from the possibility of endowing the nuclear spins with either a positive or negative temperature at will, as described in the section on the rotating reference frame. Prepared at a negative temperature, nuclear spins take up a configuration that *maximizes* their energy, generating structures never before observed or even dreamed of by the friends of Magnus' big brother.

The preparation of an ordered state involves two stages — dynamic polarization followed by ADRF. The next step is its observation with a view to determining its nature and to checking that theoretical predictions are confirmed.

For example, in the case of an antiferromagnetic state, NMR makes it possible to confirm the theory that the transverse susceptibility is independent of spin temperature whereas the longitudinal susceptibility decreases with spin temperature.

Without going into detail, let us mention that one of the substances where nuclear order has been most studied, calcium fluoride CaF_2, exhibits antiferromagnetic structures; these have been observed for several different orientations in the applied magnetic field and for both positive and negative spin temperatures and are in accord with the theory. Ferromagnetic domains have also been observed. One very productive method has been the use of the NMR of rare isotopes of low magnetic moment which, to a first approximation, do not perturb the structure appreciably. One such microscopic probe of internal structure is the rare isotope ^{43}Ca which is 0.3% abundant. This has made possible the unambiguous identification of different structures of ^{19}F spins that could not be distinguished by ^{19}F NMR alone.

One beautiful application of this nuclear probe method has been the discovery of a transverse helical phase in CaF_2. In order to appreciate the extraordinary nature of this phase it must be remembered that the structures produced by ADRF correspond to spin configurations as seen in the rotating frame. As long as they remain longitudinal, that is to say that the spins are parallel to the external field (the rotation axis of the frame), these structures maintain the same form in the laboratory frame; the structures are static.

On the other hand, transverse nuclear structure of the spins of ^{19}F has the extraordinary property that it *rotates* at the ^{19}F Larmor frequency when viewed in the laboratory frame. The reason why this structure does not dissipate energy by inducing an electromotive force in the detection coil is that by its very nature all the possible orientations in the transverse plane are equally likely, and the voltage is zero. Nevertheless the observation of coupling between these spins and those of ^{43}Ca bears out the theory and allows us to explore the structure in detail. Needless to say, no equivalent effects are possible or even imaginable in electron magnetism.

Just as with electron magnetism, the most detailed information on ordered structures of nuclear spins is provided by neutron diffraction. As explained above, the neutron "talks" not to the nuclear magnetic moment but to the pseudomagnetic moment. It is an unlucky fact that the ^{19}F nucleus, used in the much-studied CaF_2 structures, has an abnormally low pseudomagnetic moment, making it impractical for neutron study. However, after much trouble it has proved possible to produce ordered structure in lithium hydride where the enormous pseudomagnetic moment of the proton has made it possible to observe Bragg reflections from a "super-lattice" characteristic of antiferromagnetic states. The principle is this—in the absence of antiferromagnetism, two adjacent crystalline planes appear identical to neutrons, but they are recognized to be different if the nuclear spin orientations and hence the pseudomagnetic moments are opposite in the two planes, as they are in the antiferromagnetic state. The periodicity of the lattice thus appears to be doubled, which leads to additional Bragg reflections (known as superlattice reflections) which disappear above the transition temperature along with the antiferromagnetism. It was this observation of the superlattice that finally convinced the doubters of the reality of nuclear magnetic order. These followers of classical (electron) magnetism had always regarded the rotating frame and the ADRF technique with some mistrust.

We must now describe another experiment which, after several years of preparation, has finally permitted the observation of nuclear antiferromagnetic order in copper. In all respects this experiment seems to run counter to the prescriptions outlined above for CaF_2 and LiH. The sample is metallic and polycrystalline, the initial polarization is achieved by the brute force method, the adiabatic demagnetization is performed in the laboratory frame, and the detection stage uses a sensitive magnetometer called a squid, which, unlike NMR, measures static or very slowly-modulated magnetization. This difference in approach is reflected in the type of structure produced and the nature of the observations made.

A special place in the field of study of nuclear order is reserved for solid helium-3, where the effect was observed at the end of the nineteen-seventies. This follows from the fact that the interactions responsible for this order are not magnetic in nature. A similar situation is well-known in electron magnetism where these effects are called "exchange interactions" and are responsible for the existence of ferromagnetism, which has been known for centuries, and antiferromagnetism, just a half-century old. This is a quantum mechanical effect arising from the indistinguishability of atoms, and in general manifests itself in the form of a bilinear scalar coupling between electron spins, or in the case of helium-3, coupling between nuclear spins. By indistinguishability of fundamental particles we mean that there is no physical method capable of making a distinction between a process whereby two adjacent ^{3}He nuclei exchange spin orientations and one where they interchange positions keeping the same spin orientations. One could claim that the question has no sense. For the case of electron magnetism, Pierre Weiss, three-quarters of a century ago, when quantum mechanics did not exist, had the brilliant idea of explaining the properties of ferromagnetism by postulating a hypothetical local field, which he called the molecular field. This local field may have values as high as a million gauss and corresponds to temperatures of a few hundred degrees kelvin. In the case of ^{3}He the situation is complicated by the fact that one can imagine more complicated processes than simple exchange of two adjacent atoms, for example permutations of three or four atoms, corresponding to coupling of three or four spins. Nevertheless the concept of local molecular field is still useful for giving an idea of the order of magnitude of the coupling energies, and thereby, the transition temperature T_c. The latter varies by several orders of magnitude as a function of pressure (which follows from the strong pressure dependence of the overlap of the wavefunctions of neighbour nuclei, which is responsible for the exchange forces). The transition temperature is of the order of a millikelvin in the neighbourhood of the melting curve of ^{3}He corresponding to a molecular field of a few thousand gauss.

It is possible to reach this transition temperature, which is three or four orders of magnitude higher than that observed in studies of nuclear magnetic dipole order, by means of an external refrigerator without recourse to adiabatic demagnetization of the ^{3}He spins. However it is interesting to note that this external refrigerator, which allows the helium-3 to be cooled well below one millikelvin and thus below the transition temperature, uses demagnetized nuclei of metallic copper as the source of the cooling. The heat conduction from the solid helium-3 to the copper is accomplished by a heat exchanger constructed of very thin wires. The most significant and brilliant experiments have been carried out on a single crystal of helium-3; because its molecular field is so large, it is possible to apply an external magnetic field of several hundred gauss without modifying the nature of the ordered state. Some sophisticated NMR measurements as a function of orientation of the single crystal in the applied field have made it possible to make a detailed identification of the antiferromagnetic structure, which turns out to be quite unusual.

On this successful note we end the incomplete saga of Magnus' adventures as they have unfolded in just under a quarter century since the end of "The Early Years". I leave it to the younger generation to predict his progress in the next quarter century*.

* The indomitable reader, still thirsting at this stage for more knowledge of nuclear magnetism may wish to try the following references:
For Chapter 1, "The Early Years": *The Principles of Nuclear Magnetism*. A. Abragam, Oxford University Press, 1961.
For Chapter 2, "The Dawn of 1984": *Nuclear Magnetism: Order and Disorder*. A. Abragam and M. Goldman, Oxford University Press, 1982.

Atomic and Molecular Physics*

Are there enough professors in the *Collège de France* to satisfy our proud motto: *omnia docet?* For a long time I doubted it; today I believe this House is large enough, provided that it only accepts true scientists. All that is necessary is that we know how to make the right choice: first of all the discipline then the man. By tradition the two decisions are separated in time but in our minds they are inevitably indistinguishable.

This uncompromising search for quality overrides all other considerations when we make an appointment. For in two senses we have absolute freedom of choice. We are free to appoint anyone, for, despite the fact that we are short of suitable quarters, materials, technical support and all manner of things, we well know that few would refuse election to this College. We are also free to choose the discipline; we are not required to maintain any particular educational service, as they say in government circles, we are not bound, as an institution, to any formal policy, to any program of research or to any long term plan drawn up elsewhere. We are not bound by precedent: a once-prestigious professorial chair may be left unfilled if the research runs dry or the man cannot be found; by the way, the two usually go together. We have already done so more than once and we shall do it again if necessary.

Today I am proposing that we keep the Chair of Atomic and Molecular Physics, but this is by no means a case of simply reappointing a professor

* Formal report before the Assembly of the Professors of the *Collège de France* recommending an election to the Chair of Atomic and Molecular Physics, June 1972.

but rather a branching out into a completely new direction, as I shall show later.

But first of all, I hope my colleagues will bear with me for a few minutes while I take on the role of Auguste Comte and outline for you the various disciplines which go to make up physics, with a view to identifying the place of atomic and molecular physics among these other fields of study. We could base our classification on physical dimension. Suppose we begin with objects on the same scale as man; the materials that lie all about us are the subject of physics of condensed matter. These materials are made up of atoms, and of molecules, which are groupings containing a small number of atoms (except for biological molecules where the number of atoms can be very large). Atomic and molecular physics is the study of the individual properties of molecules and atoms, in isolation from each other. An atom is composed of electrons moving around a central nucleus. The size of an atom, that is to say the radius of its electronic orbitals, is of the order of one Ångstrom unit, that is to say, one ten-millionth of a millimetre.

The nucleus, of a size one hundred thousand times smaller than the atom, is made up of more elementary particles called nucleons. Nuclear physics is the study of nuclei considered as tightly-bound groups of nucleons held together by very large forces called "nuclear forces" or "strong interactions".

Finally, in addition to nucleons, there is a whole hierarchy of other, more or less unstable, particles, which interact with each other and which transform into each other. These particles were first discovered in cosmic rays before it was possible to generate them deliberately in high-energy accelerators. They have various names—hadrons or leptons, mesons or baryons, fermions or bosons—devised to emphasize one or other particular property. These particles or corpuscles, which some scientists are reluctant to call elementary particles, represent the finest subdivision of matter achievable today (1972). Their study is known as particle physics.

To the extent that nuclei are built up of nucleons, one could say that condensed matter is related to atoms in the same way that the atomic nucleus is related to its nucleons, and the nucleus is sometimes said to be made up of nuclear "matter".

Let us recapitulate: condensed matter is built up of atoms and molecules; nuclear matter is built up of particles. In going from one to the other there is an enormous change of scale, let us say in round figures a factor of a million in going from the molecule to the nucleon. There is a comparable change in the cohesive energy since atoms and molecules are held together by electromagnetic forces which are much weaker than the strong forces which hold the nucleus together.

If we take as the starting point condensed matter on the same scale as man, we can go in the other direction towards larger and larger objects—planets, stars and nebulae, where gravitational forces that are negligibly small on the atomic scale, become dominant. Here there may well be fantastic objects such as pulsars and quasars, the former possessing the enormously high density characteristic of nuclear matter and a mass equal to that of the sun but a radius of only a few kilometers, while the latter move with speeds comparable with those of particles in an accelerator, and all emitting gigantic amounts of energy. But there is too little time to imitate Pascal, fascinated by the infinitely small and the inifinitely large, so let's get back to atomic and molecular physics.

The first thirty years of this century saw a period of explosive development in this field of physics, with the brilliantly successful early quantum theory of Bohr and Sommerfeld, followed by the new mechanics of Louis de Broglie, Schrödinger, Heisenberg and Dirac, providing a more and more accurate description of the structure of atoms and molecules and their interaction with light. All the secrets of the atom appeared to be revealed and physicists turned their attention to other fields while atomic physics entered a period of fifteen to twenty years of calm if not of stagnation, depending on the country involved.

At the same time as this temporary decline in atomic physics, there came about a spectacular development of nuclear physic, followed just after the war, by particle physics. Many physicists turned towards these new, highly active areas. This was the case of Francis Perrin, the former incumbent of the Chair of Atomic and Molecular Physics, and of his colleagues who, little by little, abandoned atomic and molecular physics to devote themselves more and more to nuclear physics and particularly particle physics.

It is in this sense that I meant that to maintain the Chair of Atomic and Molecular Physics actually means that the *Collège de France* would be moving in a completely new direction.

Nevertheless, at the end of the war, atomic physics had come safely through the desert, and if we do not mind mixing metaphors, we could say that twenty-five years later it still has not reached its zenith. As so often in such cases, its progress was due to a combination of new techniques with new ideas.

The first step was the development of radiofrequency spectroscopy, begun by Rabi with his atomic beams, applied to molecules by Townes, but in particular applied to the hydrogen atom by Lamb in a historical experiment. The basic idea is very simple. Traditional (optical) spectroscopy consists in the observation of the absorption of a quantum of light, or photon, by an atom which passes from an energy state A to another energy state B. The difference in energy, or as we say the separation of the levels A and B is equal to the energy of the photon, since energy must be conserved.

If the two levels A and B are so close that their separation is less than the energy of the photon of light, traditional spectroscopy is only able to measure the separation by observing optical transitions separately from A and B to some third level C, taking the difference of energies of the corresponding two photons. It is just as if we were to measure the distance between the Arc de Triomphe and the Bastille by travelling from the Arc de Triomphe to Chicago and then from Chicago to the Bastille, obtaining the result by difference, not a very reliable procedure. Radiofrequency spectroscopy, by using photons of much lower energy, allows us to travel directly from the Arc de Triomphe to the Bastille, that is to say to measure the transition A to B directly and with an accuracy out of all proportion to that of the first method.

It was the radiofrequency techniques developed for radar during the war which made this method experimentally feasible.

Earlier I mentioned Lamb's experiment, first carried out in 1947 and repeated several times since then with ever increasing accuracy. In the development of our ideas about the interaction of light with matter, it has played a role that extends far beyond the boundaries of atomic physics, and despite its abstract character, I would like to give you an appreciation of this experiment in non-technical language by means of a rather unorthodox analogy.

But first of all let me remind you that in 1928 the English physicist Dirac put together features of the theory of relativity with quantum mechanics in order to account quantitatively for all the properties of the hydrogen atom in a rigorous and simple manner. It was not until 1947, thanks to the increased precision of radiofrequency spectroscopy that Lamb was able to show that one of energy levels of the hydrogen atom was in fact very slightly shifted with respect to the value predicted by the Dirac theory. This shift was at once explained qualitatively by the ability of the atom to emit and immediately reabsorb photons of all energies, even energies much higher than those that are available within the atom. The key point is that if reabsorption immediately follows emission before the emitted photon can be observed, conservation of energy need not apply in the intermediate state. Unfortunately the theory of quantum electrodynamics predicts that the energy level displacement due to this emission-reabsorption process should be infinite and not the very small shift measured by Lamb. The big advance in quantum theory consisted in perfecting the methods of "renormalization" which, although they still cause a few raised eyebrows among mathematicians, provide an unambiguous derivation of the very small shift in energy observed by Lamb.

In my proposed analogy, the atom is represented by a financier with two bank accounts A and B, with the two balances corresponding to the two energy states of the atom. Suppose our financier writes a cheque on account A in favour of account B for an amount that is very much larger than his entire account (this is the analogue of the emitted photon) while at the same time crediting the A account with an identical amount drawn on the second account B (this is the reabsorption of the photon). His bank manager can make no objection because neither account is overdrawn long enough for any legal action to be undertaken. An unwitting observer, seeing enormous amounts of money being paid out or cashed, might believe that the financier was immensely rich; this is the original theory which predicted an infinite result. The financial community, with inside knowledge, naturally undestand that this is all bluff but judge that our financier's true capital is only slightly affected by these fictitious transactions, partly a small debit due to overdraft charges and partly a small credit due to interest on a very large deposit. The theory of renormalization permits this difficult calculation—subtraction of two infinite quantities—to be carried out correctly.

The point to note is that the properties of an atom, and more generally those of any kind of particle, isolated in space without any radiation, are modified by what are known as vacuum fluctuations, that is to say, virtual energy exchange between the atom and empty space, producing very tiny but real effects. The atom or particle is sometimes said to be "dressed up" by these space fluctuations, thereby acquiring different properties from those of the "naked" particle.

If I seem to have gone on at length on this concept it is because I shall need to return to it towards the end of my talk.

I will say no more about radiofrequency spectroscopy which is still a very active field of atomic and molecular physics, and which has been applied by Bloch and Purcell to the study of condensed matter opening up the study of nuclear magnetism.

Another great success of atomic and molecular physics was Townes' discovery of a method for producing extremely monochromatic, directed and intense radiation by means of a device he has named the laser. Inspired by Einstein's theory of radiation, Townes showed that if an assembly of atoms could be prepared with a population inversion, that is to say a condition where the excited states of the atoms are more populated than lower energy states, then these atoms can radiate collectively in a coherent fashion, producing radiation which differs in a fundamental way from that produced by conventional light sources.

At first physicists were slow to appreciate the full importance of this marvellous physical device, to the point where some were moved to call the laser a cure looking for a disease, but those days are now long past. The incredibly narrow spectral lines emitted by the laser have completely transformed optical spectroscopy. It also provides the means of concentrating large amounts of light energy into a very restricted volume, in a very narrow bandwidth and for periods of time as short as a millionth of a millionth of a second, thereby creating a new kind of physics and opening up promising avenues for energy production by controlled fusion of light atoms*.

It is still too early to appreciate the full impact this amazing tool will have on the development of modern physics, but one thing is already certain—all the text books on optics will need to be rewritten to take account of the laser.

Now I come to the third part of my talk, the contribution made to atomic and molecular physics by the French school of Kastler and Brossel and their followers, and more recently the most brilliant among them, Claude Cohen-Tannoudji and his coworkers.

Kastler and Brossel's first discovery was the optical detection of radiofrequency transitions. When I spoke earlier of the high resolving power of radiofrequency spectroscopy—what I called the direct method of measuring the distance between the Arc de Triomphe and the Bastille—I was careful not to mention one weakness of the method, its low sensitivity. Because radiofrequency photons possess very little energy, before they can influence the detection device large numbers are required, many times more than for optical photons, and so a large number of atoms must be used. The improvement in precision is at the expense of sensitivity. The idea proposed by Kastler and Brossel was to irradiate an assembly of atoms with a beam of photons of light and simultaneously bathe them in a radiofrequency field, thus ingeniously combining the high sensitivity of the first technique with the high resolving power of the second. This procedure also lends itself quite naturally to the study of the fine structure of atoms in an excited state.

The second idea, closely related to the first, is that of optical pumping. Irradiation with polarized light makes it possible to depopulate or even completely empty certain sub-levels of the atomic ground state, while overpopulating certain other sub-levels.

I shall try to illustrate this method by an analogy. To fix our ideas, suppose that an assembly of atoms has a ground state which consists of two

* And also for ghastly space weapons (1984!).

sub-levels A and B that are initially equallly populated, and suppose that there is just a single excited state C. In our analogy there are two alpine villages A and B connected by two identical ski slopes to the summit C, common to both. Two ski-lifts carry skiers up from A and B to the summit C from where they ski down again, towards village A or village B with equal probability. If at the beginning of the afternoon equal numbers of skiers start from A and B and if the ski-lifts operate at equal rates, it is clear that at the end of the day there will be just as many at A as at B. By contrast, if the A ski-lift is working more efficiently than that from B, more skiers will end the day at village B. In fact if the B ski-lift is shut down, all the skiers will end up in village B. Now villages A and B represent the two sub-levels of the ground state. The summit C is the excited state. The ski-lifts A and B are two light beams with opposite senses of circular polarization which promote atoms from A or B to the excited state C. The descent of skiers towards A and B on a 50:50 basis represents the spontaneous emission of light from C as atoms fall back to the ground state.

The unequal efficiencies of the two ski-lifts correspond to different intensities for the two incident polarized light beams. Shutting down one ski-lift completely is equivalent to extinguishing the corresponding light beam. By emptying the state A at the expense of state B, we create a situation which differs profoundly from that of thermodynamic equilibrium, and this allows us to make very precise measurements of the fine structure of the atom.

These techniques, now used worldwide, have revolutionized the study of a large number of atomic parameters. Their systematic application to molecules is only just beginning.

In closing I would like to describe one of the elegant methods due to Cohen-Tannoudji, that is the "dressing" of the atom by a beam of photons of light or photons of radiofrequency radiation.

Let me remind you again of the story of our financier friend in the Lamb experiment, who had no other resources except his two bank accounts A and B between which he played his little game of deposit and withdrawal. Let us suppose that he enters into a conspiracy with a large financial organization which agrees to make some extremely large transfers to his account on the condition that he agrees to pay them back at once. Clearly the situation resembles that when the financier worked on his own, his financial standing would seem to be increased to an extent that depended on the nature and frequency of the short-term loans made by his accomplices. The equivalent experiment in physics is that of an atom, not in free space, but in an intense applied radiation field. Although the photons from this field are re-emitted as soon as they are absorbed, this does not mean that they do not modify the optical and magnetic properties of the atom in a quite profound way. Cohen-Tannoudji and his students were able to derive the complete theory of these unique experiments and confirm them quantitatively in considerable detail. The great physicist Ludwig Boltzmann was sometimes criticized for the heavy methods that he used. He habitually replied "I leave elegance to the tailors." Despite my admiration for this great physicist I have to admit to a weakness for elegance in physics, particularly when it does not exclude efficiency, and I pay tribute to it here.

I am convinced that there are many beautiful experiments still to be done in atomic and molecular physics.

Big Science versus Little Science*

At the end of the last war, physics in France was at its lowest. The holocaust of the First World War, where a whole generation of young scientists had fallen as infantry officers, had already started a decline which in spite of the impact of brilliant individuals like Louis de Broglie and Frédéric Joliot was acutely felt by those who, like myself, were attempting to start research just before the Second World War. The antiquated structures of the French University, the divorce between experiment and theory, the scarcity of supervisors able and willing to give to a beginner the guidance he required, the incredible poverty of most laboratories, acted as an efficient deterrent for those foolhardy enough to attempt a career in research. Whether I would have succeeded under those conditions remains an unanswered question; war and German occupation put, for six years, a stop to all my endeavours in the field of research. I was given a second chance however. The leaders of the French Atomic Energy Commission which was created in late 1945, and where I had found a job in 1946, had the foresight to realize that the only way for our country to regain a foothold in science was to send young people to the places where science had not stopped, namely America and Britain.

I was found young enough to qualify and this is how, having chosen Britain and Oxford, I came in 1948 to the Clarendon Laboratory. Little did

---

* Ninth Cherwell-Simon lecture, Oxford, 15 October 1968.

I expect upon entering this laboratory, where Cherwell had had the wisdom to bring Simon fifteen years earlier, that twenty years later I would have the great honour to deliver the Cherwell-Simon lecture. I think I can say that the two years I spent at the Clarendon Laboratory were the happiest in my whole life. For the first time I had found the stimulating scientific environment I had been yearning for all my life. This is not the place to thank all those who helped me in my late, but not too late, apprenticeship of science, but I must name the two men who really taught me the meaning of creative work in physics : Maurice Pryce and Brebis Bleaney. And since it was Cherwell and Simon who made the Clarendon the place where such things were possible it is not unfitting that I express here my deep personal gratitude to both of them.

When I rashly undertook to prepare a lecture dealing in general terms with some of the problems facing the physicists of our time I was not aware of the staggering amount of learned literature concerned with all the aspects of what is generally described as Science Policy. Upon perusal of a very small part of this literature I discovered to my dismay that all the thoughts that had occured to me from time to time on these subjects both as a physicist and, during the latter part of my career, as so-called research leader, had been expressed many times in a much more forceful manner than I could ever hope to achieve.

My only excuse for inflicting upon you the results of my cogitations and observations is that, trivial as they may be, they have come to me as the result of my own experience.

At the end of the war and for a few years afterwards the main preoccupation in science policy seems to have been the responsibility of the scientist in connection with the bomb. Physicists who had never had anything to do with it in the past and were unlikely to do so in the future, who had never seen an atom bomb and would not know one from a portable gramophone, were asked by anxious journalists about their views on the problem and explained at great length how they would deal with it.

Later the interest shifted to peaceful applications of nuclear energy; it was recognized eventually that the main problems there were of making large boilers and long tubes that would not leak, clog, jam, rust, split, rot, melt or burst and that sophisticated atomic and nuclear physicists had very little to say on the subject.

During a period which may have started ten years ago a new concept appeared which is still going strong: planning research.

How much research should a country undertake, how much of it basic and how much applied, should it be done in the universities, in government establishements, or in industry and in what proportions? How much physics, how much chemistry, how much biology, how much oceanography, metallurgy or astronomy. Then in physics: how much high energy physics, low energy nuclear physics, solid state physics, optics, thermodynamics, quantum electronics, etc. etc.?

How many Ph.Ds should one produce per year in each field, where would they go, how long should they stay in one place, should they change their field in the course of their career and if so how often? What is the optimum rate of growth in each discipline, what research should be done on an international rather than national level?

Those, and many many more, are the important questions hotly debated by all those who have, or think they have, a say in the establishment of science policy, such as government advisors, directors of research, department heads, group leaders, senior scientists, educators, scientific journalists, members of various panels and eventually practically all members of the scientific community over thirty.

And all the time in the background lurks what, if we were in America, I might call the green-eyed monster which calls the tune: I mean money.

Science has become big. It employs large numbers of people, requires large and complicated equipment and costs large sums of money: this is the inescapable truth. I would like to examine in the course of this talk some of the implications, consequences and dangers of this situation.

I will be concerned with fundamental research only. Now comes the usual tedious argument: what exactly does one mean by fundamental research and where does one draw the line between it and applied research? It is sometimes claimed that there is no sharp division between fundamental and applied research where people with similar backgrounds use similar equipment in similar surroundings to do very similar work. I beg to differ with this view: there is a very large difference and it is in the choice of the problems.

In fundamental research the aim is to understand the laws of nature: the phenomenon to be studied must therefore be as simple and as general as possible. Thus, in solid state physics for instance, (where the distinction with applied research is least sharp) one would choose a sample of great chemical and sometimes isotopical purity with a simple and well-known crystal structure and a simple geometrical shape if surface effects are important. Having thus discarded as many unessential complications as possible one should not be content with less than a full understanding of the phenomena under study.

In applied research the aim is to produce eventually a useful device: full understanding of what goes on may be a help, but need not be a necessity. The choice of the substance on the other hand may be dictated by technical and economical considerations often incompatible with the simplicity of structure which leads to a better understanding of the pheno-menon. For instance it is very essential in nuclear technology to know the effects of nuclear radiations on artificial graphite, a complicated and ill-defined substance, used as a moderator in some types of reactors. For a fundamental study of radiation damage, diamond is a better substance although it may not be economical to use it as a moderator in a large reactor. It could happen that the diamond industry would see a practical interest in the change of coloration that irradiation induces in a diamond. The same study would then immediatly become applied science. It is all in the intent as the Church teaches us.

Every student of French literature has been taught that the reason our classical tragedy deals with people of exalted rank, kings and princesses, is a highly intellectual one: the interplay of great passions, love, hate, pity, jealousy, will appear more clearly and can be studied much more efficiently if unessentials such as the necessity of earning a living by tilling the land or going to the office are removed. In this sense one can say that fundamental research is the classical tragedy whilst the modern drama where men have professions and obligations besides giving free course to their passions would by the same token correspond to applied research.

Let us take up now a field which today is in the forefront of fundamental research, high energy physics. It is pure tragedy in the sense of our definition and it is big all right. An analysis of its present trends should be most instructive for the understanding of the workings of big science. Everybody knows why high energy physics is important. It deals with the innermost core of the physical world and the laws it strives to understand and formulate are at the bottom of everything. In spite of the important progress achieved recently in that field, in spite of the discovery of some remarkable regularities in the realm of elementary particles, regularities describable in terms of attractive mathematical schemes, in spite of the orderly classification which has replaced the chaos of a few years ago, we still do not know, we do not understand the basic laws of the world of elementary particles. And in a certain sense as long as *this* is not understood, *nothing* will be fully understood. However exciting some branches of modern science developing at a breath taking rate: be it superconductivity, lasers, Mössbauer effect, cybernetics, astrophysics, space physics, even molecular biology, in my view none of these cut as deep as the field of elementary particles. This is enough to explain the attraction of this discipline, year after year and all over the world, on some of the most gifted among the young physicists.

So much for the ends, what about the means. The first problem is to produce particles of very high energy by means of devices known as accelerators, which are very big things indeed. Let me remind you that one of the smallest and oldest of high energy machines, Saturne at Saclay, completed ten years ago, has a diameter of 18 meters for a top energy of 3 Bev (or billions of electron volts). The CERN and Brookhaven machines with 30 Bev have diameters ten times as large, the Soviet machine just completed at Serpukhov with a top energy of 80 Bev has a diameter of 500 meters and the Weston machine under construction in the United States now, will have a diameter of 2,500 meters for a top energy of 400 Bev. For the cost of these machines a million dollars per Bev is a useful rule of thumb. Do not believe however that when you have built the accelerator you are through. There are actually four successive steps in high energy physics experimentation.

After the acceleration, just described, comes the detection where the same escalation occurs as with accelerators. One of the most important tools there is the hydrogen bubble chamber, where the paths of charged particles are materialized by strings of bubbles which appear along these paths, and can be photographed. The bubble chambers are placed in magnetic fields which curve the trajectories of charged particles by an amount that depends on their energy, enabling it to be measured. The first bubble chambers of a decade ago had volumes of a few litres. The largest British hydrogen chamber has a volume of 250 litres, the largest French chamber a volume of 180 litres, the largest chamber at CERN a volume of 500 litres. The British are planning a chamber of 2,500 litres, we are building one of 6,000 litres to be installed near the Serpukhow machine in early 1970. CERN together with Germany and France are building a chamber of 20,000 litres. Need I tell you that the United States are not staying behind, their largest project having a volume of 46,000 litres? There are no simple rules for the cost; I shall just mention that the cost of the big CERN chamber will be of the same order as the original cost of building the CERN accelerator.

Although less costly per unit than bubble chambers, other detection devices such as counters, spark-chambers, polarized targets, on-line computers, etc. which require a considerable amount of very sophisticated electronics contribute a comparable amount to the detection bill. Next comes the analysis of results, mainly scanning and measuring of photographs. This is a tremendous task again. Millions of photographs are taken each year in bubble chambers or spark chambers and must be processed. Special scanning and measuring tables manned, (if that is the right word) by specially trained girls, of increasing sophistication (the tables not the girls) can be found by the dozen in every high energy laboratory. Our laboratory at Saclay, probably the largest in France, employs approximately 200 girls (working part time) to scan and measure the photographs. There is everywhere a strong trend toward automation, replacing manual labour with automatic devices with a far higher processing speed. These devices with electronic, optical and mechanical components of high complexity and precision are costly too. A machine called HPD (from the initials of its inventors) costs around 4 million francs and major high energy laboratories have more than one.

Last but not least comes His Majesty, the high speed computer, where all the data are fed. It represents one of the largest items in the running costs of high energy laboratories.

Let me indicate that last year our high energy laboratory has used 6,000 hours of IBM 7094 which was about half all the computing done at Saclay for all the departments.

Although the best known example of "Big Science", high energy physics is far from being the only one.

Let me dismiss, rapidly space research even costlier than high energy physics which has really very little to do with fundamental research. It is not a tragedy as we have defined it, even though some may think that it is one in the usual sense.

Nuclear physics as distinct from high energy or elementary particle physics, uses equipment sufficiently heavy and expensive to justify its belonging to Big Science. For instance, the linear electron accelerator built at Saclay for nuclear structure studies, which has a large duty cycle, a very good energy resolution, and very high intensity, with an average beam power over 100 kilowatts, will have cost, for the machine only, over 40 million francs and about as much for the buildings, radiation shielding and scientific equipment.

Solid state physics, traditionally belonging to "Little Science", has moved into the big league too. The costliest instruments are the high flux reactors which provide collimated beams of slow neutrons, a wonderful tool for exploring the structure and the dynamics of matter in bulk. The high flux reactor being built for physicists by France and Germany in Grenoble will cost over 200 million francs.

Specialized laboratories where high magnetic fields are produced by conventional or superconducting magnets are also costly enough to qualify as Big Science.

Finally it should be remembered that many typically Little Science studies such as Mössbauer effect, oriented radioactive nuclei, optical pumping, etc., would not be possible without the existence of large equipments such as isotopic separators, atomic reactors or cyclotrons.

Researches on plasma physics and controlled fusion offer an interesting and unusual example of an applied research returning to fundamental research. As the saying goes: "this is a non-profit organization but we did not plan it that way". After many unsuccessful attempts to realize controlled fusion it became clear that a much better understanding of the elementary processes taking place in a hot plasma was necessary before one could begin to think of confining it, at sufficiently high temperatures and densities and for a sufficiently long time, for controlled fusion to occur. What gives to these studies their character of Big Science is the necessity to make large scale experiments in very strong magnetic fields if one wants them to be "clean" experiments, capable of a quantitative theoretical description. To give the scale of the experiments let me say that in a machine presently under study in France and called "superstator" it is planned to confine a plasma for a fraction of a second in a volume where a magnetic energy of 60 megajoules is being stored. The cost of the machine will be 30 million francs.

In this review of Big Science I have arbitrarily limited myself to disciplines pursued in our own laboratories omitting important and costly studies such as radioastronomy.

Before we consider the problems that the existence of Big Science, such as it appears from the outline given above, poses to the scientific community and to the society at large, let me say this: It is quite clear that the main task of the physicist, understanding the structure of the physical world, will not be achieved without Big Science. Bright theories and clever ideas are welcome, indeed are necessary, but they are just not enough at the present stage of development of science. If the means for pursuing Big Science are not forthcoming, an individual scientist, a group of scientists, can switch to the less expensive, and to my personal taste, more attractive fields of Little Science, such as those practised so successfully in this laboratory; indeed a bright physicist is more likely to reap the rewards of his ability in the fields of Little Science, as can be seen from a perusal of the list of Nobel Prize winners. This may solve his personal problems but the main problems of understanding our universe will remain largely unsolved.

The main problem of Big Science is easy to spell out: it is money. I shall be brief about it: not because it is unimportant, far from it, but rather because its very importance has caused it to be so widely discussed that the main arguments pro and contra are familiar to everyone.

Let me give you some figures, very approximate, but perhaps sufficient for an order of magnitude discussion. The yearly expense for fundamental research in Western Europe is around 5 billion francs which sounds impressive but which is only one third of a percent of the sum of the gross national products of all the countries. Is it too much and would it break Western Europe financially even if eventually it approached the asymptotic value of one percent? I wonder. It is difficult to discuss these things without making some assumptions about the sanity of our world. Is 400 million dollars spread over seven years too much for the American super high energy accelerator when 20 billion dollars are spent every year on the Vietnam war. Is 5 billion francs per year too much for basic research in the whole of Western Europe when the Common Market countries propose to spend 4 billion francs a year to keep, through subsidies, at their present level the prices paid to the farmers for milk and butter. How does the British participation to the European 300 Bev machine, of the order of 40 million pounds compare with the net loss caused to the economy of your country by the brain drain? I do not know but perhaps you do, and if you don't you might want to find out.

In the meantime, people and governments being what they are and money being tight, an argument often heard is that in the interest of the community one should support applied research and development rather than fundamental research and that for the latter the branches capable of producing useful results for technology should be singled out for support. Methods known as cost analysis, evolved in industry, are extrapolated to fundamental research to separate the sheep from the goats. With respect to the cost analysis system may I recall to those of you who have not heard it before the story of the efficiency experts entrusted with the task of evaluating the rentability of the various components of the French railway trains. They found that first and second class carriages, considering their passenger load and the cost of the tickets, were paying their way, that the same was true to a lesser extent of sleeping cars because of a lesser occupancy and that the dining cars which were breaking about even, should be kept because of the convenience to the public. But they discovered that all trains had at the front (or exceptionally at the back) a heavy vehicle which carried neither goods nor passengers with the exception of one or two people, who not only did not pay their fare but were actually *given* money by the company. The financial utility of this vehicle was clearly nil and it was proposed to do away with it.

May I suggest that with respect to the train of technology, fundamental research plays the role of this unwanted vehicle.

A few years ago as I was visiting a research laboratory in Southern California belonging to a large industrial firm, I was told by the head of the laboratory: "You understand of course that this lab with a research budget of one million dollars is a very small part of our activity. The real business is transacted further north in our big plant near San Diego and there, it is one hundred million dollars that we lose every year".

And then, how does one know in advance which branch of fundamental research is most likely to have technologically useful developments? The unfortunate pronouncement of Lord Rutherford back in 1933 "Anyone who expects a source of power from the transformations of these atoms is talking moonshine", thanks to high-energy physicists, eager to defend the potential practical usefulness of their field, has probably become the most quoted of Rutherford's statements, which is rather unfair. But so many other examples of unexpected and important practical applications of results of fundamental research could be given from Hertz and Roentgen to Bloch, Purcell and Townes that it is hardly necessary to belabour this point.

One last point about Big Science and money. Research on a large scale is not something that you can turn off during the lean years and on again during the fat years. When you turn it off you turn it off for good. An irreversible process takes place, the research workers change their field or they change their country and the price to pay for starting again is much higher than the savings made during the stoppage.

Have I given the impression that I am an unconditional supporter of Big Science? I hope not, because speaking as a physicist I am acutely aware of the risks of corruption that it brings to the soul of our community.

In order to obtain the large sums of money necessary for the projects of Big Science the scientists must convince people who have an influence in government circles or on the public opinion of the validity of their demands, which in view of the large sums involved is only proper. There is however a danger: the reasons which motivate the projects for the scientist are not always the most cogent for the layman he is trying to convince and this gives rise to what I believe is called double-think. All too often it is the very bigness of the project, striking the imagination of the public, rather than its real usefulness to the progress of science, that is being put forward. And the hard-headed civil servants from the Ministry of Finance, even if their imaginations are not too easy to inflame, like the idea of their money (it is not theirs really but they think it is) buying a nice big chunk of hardware housed in a large building.

Fundamental science is international, scientists working all over the world on the same subject speak the same language* and communicate

---

* Broken English.

freely with each other. It is a nice thought and what is more it is true. It is all the more regrettable that in each country the most effective argument that scientists can use to get money from their governments is "we cannot afford to fall behind the fellow next door". The statement of Professor McMillan of Berkeley that I lift rather unfairly from his testimony during congressional hearings on high-energy physics research: "The United States is very clearly on top of the heap", illustrates my meaning.

Between budgetary demands it is necessary, is it not, to convince the government and the public that their money has been put to good use and that great discoveries have been made. And this is how you happen to read about these discoveries in *The New York Times*, *The Observer* or the *Figaro* before they have even been accepted for publication in *Physical Review Letters*. You understand of course that the scientist who seeks such large publicity for his discoveries does so in the general interest of science, or with the more immediate but very respectable goal of getting material support for his laboratory. His modesty suffers but he is willing to lay his sufferings on the altar of science. He may be sincere in saying this, he most likely is, but the heady wine of press conferences intoxicates his innocent brain until he becomes an addict, always on the look-out for the journalists. The danger there is not so much of a scientist making a fool of himself (we have so many other opportunities to do that). It lies in the fact that through a clever salesmanship to the public opinion, backed up by an effective lobbying in the right circles, it is not always the most deserving project that gets the largest support. This happens very seldom, I am glad to say, but it can happen.

From what has just been said it appears clearly that scientists cannot be trusted unconditionally with the management of science. The governments understand it very well and this is why they give us civil servants to help us with the task. Since the war, the French ministries have been populated with a new breed of civil servants which come from the ENA or the École Nationale d'Administration, appropriately called the "Énarques". In this school, where they enter through a stiff competitive examination, they learn everything about administration and management. The most ambitious supplement this training with a diploma from the École Polytechnique where they receive a solid grounding in mathematics and a knowledge of the latest discoveries in physics due to Ampère, Arago, Cavendish and Lord Kelvin.

They are intelligent, hard-working, ambitious, scrupulously honest, (one remembers with nostalgia the phrase of Evelyn Waugh: "a vast bureaucracy... humanised by corruption") and they know everything. They sit together with us on committees where the various questions that I have listed at the beginning of this talk are being debated, in order to determine the national science policy or rather to write reports on which the government is supposed to base its science policy. It is probably a good thing that responsible scientists sit on these committees, if only to prevent the bright *Énarques* from reaching some revolutionnary conclusions. One of their "bêtes noires" is duplication: the idea that the same research could be pursued by two different teams. It is a good thing that in 1946 Bloch and Purcell did not know about it or they would not have dared to discover simultaneously the phenomenon of Nuclear Magnetic Resonance. But how frequent, how numerous, how dull and above all, how time-consuming are these committees. You need to be a scientist to bring a valuable contribution to these sessions, but if you sit there too long you stop being a scientist. Sometime ago during a reception following a conference in Soviet Russia, I got talking to a Russian whom I had not met before. He asked me what my job was and when I answered that I was Director of the Physics Division in the French Atomic Energy Commission he said: Well, I am not a physicist either, I am with the Ministry so-and-so. At first I was greatly amused by this misunderstanding but then I got the uncomfortable feeling that maybe it was not so funny after all.

Another drawback of the large projects of Big Science is that they take so long to come into being. Once the scientists have got a clear idea of what they want, after the long reports to various committes, after the protracted lobbying to get the money for the preliminary study and then for the actual construction, it takes several years before the thing is ready to operate. There is always the risk, which one must face, for otherwise one would never do anything, that the progress of science or technology will make the project obsolete or at least less interesting before it is completed. The CERN physicists were lucky that their project of a large accelerator was at its very beginning in 1952 when the technique of the strong focussing came into being, enabling them to make full use of its marvellous possibilities. The Russians were not so lucky with the Dubna machine started in 1949 and completed in 1957, with the now obsolete technique of weak focussing.

To a lesser extent there are similar difficulties with the experimentation around these big machines. The preparation of an experiment can easily take a full year or more and then the analysis of its results about as long. Because the technological aspects of these experiments are so involved it is not uncommon to have teams of twenty or thirty physicists on a single experiment. Each one of them is responsible for a small part of the experiment and one would like to think that all of them and not only the group leader, get a clear idea and an overall view of the whole experiment. Recently I came across an experiment described in *Physics Letters* where the results consisted in twenty-eight experimental points and there were twenty-nine coauthors to the article. When the technological aspects of an experiment become so complex as to require the undivided attention of the experimentalist there is always the danger of his getting so immersed in technology as to forget physics altogether.

For instance when you talk to bubble-chamber specialists who do a lot of scanning and analysing of photographs and of programming and computing, you sometimes get the impression that their real field is automation and computing rather than high energy physics. I am not saying that they are forgetting their goal, the study of elementary particles, all I am saying is that they have a hard time not to. Yet another danger faces the physicist working around these big machines: conformity. What I mean by this is the following: only a limited amount of experiments can be performed simultaneously around a large accelerator. Because each experiment is lengthy and costly, great care must be exercised in selecting among the numerous proposals those which will actually be carried out. The selection is made by committes of competent physicists (no *Énarques* there) and there is not the slightest doubt that it is absolutely fair and based on the merit of the proposals only. The fact remains however that some very interesting experiments but which have only a slender chance of success, "crazy" experiments as they are sometimes called, are usually turned down in fairness to competing proposals established on much firmer ground. The outcome is that there is a tendency to weed out "crazy" experiments and to accept "safe" experiments. I would like to remind you that when Mössbauer first discovered the effect which bears his name namely the recoilless emission of γ-rays in crystals, two American laboratories repeated his experiment, with the *same* radioactive nucleus that was used by Mössbauer rather than trying to extend his results to other nuclei. The actual reason was that they simply did not believe his results and sought to disprove them. If Mössbauer's original experiment had been of the Big Science type I doubt very much that the competent committee would have authorized it.

To conclude, I would like to mention three problems which affect the present rapid development of science and where in a certain sense Big Science is a state of mind rather than a matter of size and cost of scientific equipment.

My first point has to do with excessive specialization. Professor Van Vleck in his Cherwell-Simon lecture of a few years ago has spoken eloquently against the crass ignorance of science among people who have received an exlusively liberal education. I am sorry to say that the ignorance of some young physicists of to-day in matters even slightly remote from their own field is appalling. I was amazed to discover that some young theorists well versed in dynamics of elementary particles had never heard of the electronic band structure of metals and conversely some solid state physicists although they had heard the words, quarks, SU_3, non-conservation of CP, etc., had no idea of what they meant. I think this mutual ignorance is deplorable: physical science is one of the highest forms of culture and some of the schemes it has evolved to explain the natural phenomena are so beautiful as to give to those able to understand them a high esthetical pleasure. It seems a great pity that physicists who are fortunate in possessing the training which gives them the key to all the beauties of their science should make such a narrow use of it. The excuse sometimes given for such narrow specialization and not completely invalid, is that it is the price to pay for creativity. Physics is too hard and life too short to indulge in the contemplation of results outside of one's own field. Were it true, the price of creativity would be very high indeed, and I am not sure it is true. I think on the contrary that a knowledge of more than one discipline can be extremely fruitful and lead to new discoveries. Let me again draw an example from the Mössbauer effect. Crystallographers had known for a long time that X-ray photons could be scattered by the atoms of a crystal coherently, that is without recoil of the scattering atoms, and it is well known that a scattering can be described as an absorption followed by an emission. If nuclear physicists concerned with the recoil of radioactive nuclei emitting γ-rays had been aware of this fact, the great discovery of Mössbauer, the recoilless emission and absorption of γ-rays, could have been made much earlier.

The second point I wish to mention is the publications explosion. This is a problem about which I feel rather strongly. The number and the size of scientific publications is growing beyond the bounds of reason, making communication between scientists, which is an essential condition of scientific progress, nearly impossible. Someone has calculated that if this growth continued at its present rate, hundred years hence the velocity of progression of the front page of *Physical Review* on the library shelves would exceed the velocity of light. The relativity principle, he remarked, would not be violated since this progression actually carries no information. The trouble of course is that the number of *good* papers is increasing very slowly if at all. One is reminded of the conversation in Voltaire's novel: "Monsieur, how many plays do you have in France?" asked Candide. "Five or six thousand". "C'est beaucoup" said Candide. "How many are good?". "Fifteen or sixteen". "C'est beaucoup" said Martin. It is not that all the other papers are frankly bad, they are indifferent. As Pauli once angrily remarked about a paper that he was asked to referee: "It is not even wrong"! Not so long ago I used to browse through the summaries of all the articles in *Physical Review*. Now I have barely the time to read the titles of the articles on the back page before the next issue arrives. I feel like the attendant in a delightful cartoon of the late Peter Arno, filling a huge

Cadillac and asking the driver to switch off the engine: "You are gaining on me Sir". Various proposals have been put forward most of them making use of computers to handle the rising flood of publication (I would rather not use the word information).

One of the most ridiculous suggestions was the so-called citation index. By means of computers you could form an opinion about scientist A by finding out how many times his papers were cited by other scientists (including himself). This suggestion raises some interesting questions. There should be a weight attached to the quality of author B, who cites A, which can only be determined by counting how many people cite B. These are weighed in their turn, etc. Nice little topological problems could be considered. Given two physicists A and Z at random can you relate them by a string of continuous citations, etc.? At no time was it suggested that to find out what physicist A is worth, one could read his papers. The publication explosion is an artificial problem caused by the social pressure put on the scientist and especially on the young scientist at the beginning of his career to force him to publish. Publish now, think later! Publish or perish! these are the slogans which govern our scientific community. I have little doubt that by releasing this pressure to the extent that a scientist could without jeopardizing his career publish only when he had something to say, would improve the quality and decrease the quantity of published matter, a double boon.

The last problem is what the *Énarques* call "external mobility of scientific manpower" or in other words: "should scientific research be a life-time job?" Personally, I think not, at least for a majority of scientific workers. There is little doubt that Big Science in particular, which requires large teams, but also Little Science, simply could not progress without the young graduate students working for a Ph.D. If their supervisor is not a bad physicist and if the equipment and scientific environment are adequate, the large majority of those who choose to work for a Ph.D. do make a useful contribution to science and what is just as important enjoy themselves, and this goes probably for most of them in the first few years of post-doctoral research. I am not at all convinced that the same proportion remains valid over a certain age limit which I would hate to state arbitrarily but which is certainly below forty and probably much less. I dislike using big words but fundamental research does require in order to be successful a certain amount of inspiration, and when the fires of youth are extinguished (and the guidance of the supervisor is gone) most people just have not got it.

Someone spoke once of the ordeal of getting the Nobel Prize too young (an ordeal that, thankfully, most of us here have been spared) which, on an altogether different scale, to be sure, referred to the lack of inspiration following a youthful flash of genius. Replace genius by talent and you get the situation of many research workers dissatisfied with their position and their work. What is to be done then to insure what I might call the outgoing flux paralleling the input of fresh talent and enthusiasm which is needed? Teaching in the universities is a solution but very incomplete. In our present society at least there are just not enough teaching jobs for all and what is more all are not suited for these jobs. What then? You all know the magic word, industry, and indeed industry could help us solve of our problems while solving some of its own. Industry leaders at least in our country like to hire their staff young, just after they get their degree form one of our "Grandes Écoles" at an average age of 22-23, and to mould them as they see fit for the job on hand. It is my contention that a young Ph.D. who has done work in fundamental research for a thesis, on a subject not necessarily connected with the programme of the industry, and aged say 26 to 28, will, after an adaptation period, which should not exceed one year, be just as useful, if not more, to his employer, than a man his age, who has been hired five years earlier. Personally I would not be shocked if the government reimbursed to the employer a sizeable fraction of the salary that he paid to the young Ph.D. during the first year of his employment, when he adapts himself to the job.

In order for such a scheme, largely untried so far, to have some chance of success a double psychological barrier must be broken. Firstly the industrialist must be persuaded that one does not try to palm off on him somebody thrown out of research because he is hopeless, and it better be true.

Then the research worker should understand that there is nothing humiliating in going to work for industry after having contributed his part to the progress of science, and having acquired a training which will make him capable of handling new and unexpected problems.

If both protagonists can be persuaded that this is a normal and honourable solution rather than a desperate expedient, and if the circumstances are such that it happens to be true, some of the problems faced by scientific research will be solved.

I have touched in the foregoing on some of the problems raised by the rapid development of science. My only reason for limiting myself to fundamental research in physics and leaving out completely the vast problems of applied science and technology was the wish to keep away from problems where I have no first-hand knowledge.

I am afraid I may have given to some of you very conflicting ideas about Big Science versus Little Science. The explanation, I am sorry to say, is that the conflict is in my own mind. My rather lame conclusion would be the following: nowadays physicists cannot achieve their goal, which is understanding the universe, without Big Science. They should pursue it, seek the means it requires and convince the rest of the society to give these means to them. But to put it bluntly, they must be very careful not to lose their soul in the meantime and *propter vitam, vitae perdere causas*.

Big Science versus Little Science

POSTSCRIPT

Since this text was written in 1968, more than fifteen years have elapsed, bringing with them profound changes in the economy, in technology and in science. The price of oil has increased tenfold, economic growth has been stopped in Western countries, unemployment has replaced full employment, the technology of Japan inundates the world with its products, if not with its ideas, the development of miniaturized electronics and computers of all sizes has had consequences comparable to those of the first industrial revolution, and basic science has made great strides. One may well ask whether "Big Science versus Little Science" offers more than an outdated picture of past reality. If, in my view it has retained some validity it is because it depicts attitudes rather than facts—attitudes of the public, of political bodies, of the scientists themselves toward science, and because these attitudes have not changed much.

This postscript should be considered as a collection of footnotes accompanying the preceding text and stressing the persistence of certain attitudes, including my own, together with the more notable changes. There will be no reference to research budgets; the unformulated message of my anonymous Soviet interlocutor eventually got through to me, loud and clear, and it has been a long time since I have concerned myself with administrative and financial matters *.

* See "Return to the Fold".

I do not want to mention here, even slightly, the terrible problem of nuclear weapons, unless it be to say that the levity with which I referred to it seems out of place today.

The wide circle of the members of the scientific community who take part in the everlasting debate on the planning of research is wider today; the limitation to those over thirty holds no more. In spite of all efforts to the contrary, the confusion between basic and applied research is still entertained by many and reinforced by a few.

Let us come to high energy physics, the epitome of Big Science. Gigantism thrives more than ever. We left off at the construction in the United States of the Weston accelerator with a diameter of 2500 metres. It was completed long ago and under the name of Fermilab is a source of satisfaction to its users. Its energy, initially 300 Gev, has recently been tripled by replacing iron magnets with superconductors. A machine of similar size has been functioning now for several years at CERN in Geneva with great success. The future electron-positron collision ring under construction at CERN will have a diameter of 9 kilometres. True, the bubble chambers have stopped their impressive growth, but a large detector in operation at CERN, which houses a magnetic field of 8000 gauss in a volume of 80 cubic metres and weighs 2000 tons is a nice Brobdignagian toy. As for His Majesty the fast computer which processes the data, thanks to advances in microelectronics, it is not his size that matters but the computing power which has grown in a ratio comparable to that between the atomic bomb and conventional explosives. I made some ironic comments on an experiment with twenty-nine coauthors and twenty-eight experimental data points. In 1983, there were one hundred and thirty-six authors at CERN combining their efforts to detect barely a dozen significant events.

And yet it would be a grievous error to say, *Plus ça change, plus c'est la même chose*. During the last twelve years or so there has been an extraordinary breakthrough in particle physics, both in theory and experiment, which is still in progress as these lines are being written. The work of the hundred and thirty-six has led to the discovery of the W and Z bosons, a key prediction of the theory, and was crowned by the Nobel Prize (not for all the one hundred and thirty-six, but just two). I had said fifteen years ago, "We still do not know, we do not understand the fundamental laws of the world of elementary particles". It seems that this is not so anymore, and that if we still do not understand everything, we understand quite a lot. It is not extravagant to dream that before the end of this millenium, which is just around the corner, the young science students who graduate now will understand everything in the field of elementary particles the way they understand today (at least one hopes so) the classical laws of electromagnetism.

Taxpayers of all countries rejoice, you will be getting your money's worth.

I had considered as negligible the contribution of space activities to fundamental research; this contribution, while still the same small proportion of the space budget, has grown considerably as the budget itself expanded, something like the one percent deductible for charities.

Controlled fusion, another branch of Big Science, has grown bigger. The French "Superstator" whose construction I had announced, failed to see the light of day. It has been replaced by a machine of similar size, the Tokamac, whose name is an acronym of Russian origin and which is but a link in the chain of bigger and bigger machines of that type. The latest in Europe the JET (Joint European Torus) has just been completed. It weighs over 2000 tons and is (so far) the largest in the world. This machine, together with others of similar size in the United States and the Soviet Union, is expected to demonstrate before the end of the millenium the feasibility of building nuclear fusion reactors as energy sources. It will then remain to be seen during which part of the next millenium the nuclear fusion energy will drive out all other energy sources as hoped by its promoters. Besides this quest for nuclear fusion through the magnetic confinement of plasma, one should mention studies on dense plasmas.

There, pellets of hydrogenated or deuterated matter are shot at by powerful lasers. While the pellets are small, the lasers are gigantic and this line of research is just as much "Big Science" as magnetic confinement.

Although both this text and the previous one are in principle devoted to physics only, it is impossible not to mention the explosion (the word is not too strong) of molecular biology. Thirty years after the double helix, fiteen years after the start of genetic engineering, molecular biology is unmistakeably "Big Science". Not so much by the size and cost of its equipment, although among these one finds high flux reactors, ultracentrifuges, X-ray spectrographs, the costliest NMR and infrared spectrometers, as by the ever-growing number of research workers, and above all by the vast implications of the results, be they medical, social or even financial.

In spite of certain appearances, there is little change in the way that governments, ours in particular, administer the research that they finance. Our *Énarques* are still here, and if their well-bred gray-flannelled appearance has turned slightly pink, there are no observable effects. It is only fair to mention that in the teaching of physics at the École Polytechnique there has been a real change. Thanks to the talent and enthusiasm of a few young professors it has been completely renewed and compares favourably with leading American universities.

No changes in the pullulation of scientific publications. The wavefront of the *Physical Review* on the library shelves progresses faster than ever and each issue resembles more and more a telephone directory by its dimensions (and not only by its dimensions according to some slanderers).

The prospects for young research workers in industry has improved. This is partly due to the intelligent initiative of a few scientists well connected with both university and industry, between which they have established useful links. There is a more general reason which is a change in the outlook of the industrialists themselves. Unable to compete with the low salaries of the industries of South-East Asia, some of them have taken their chance in high technology which requires personnel with a good scientific training.

To conclude this dusting off of "Big Science versus Little Science" one should mention the recent trend of theoretical physics, traditionally "little" by its very nature, which expands and grows "big" in the dreamland of what are commonly known as simulation methods. In these methods, the statistical behaviour of a large number of interacting particles is studied by replacing the physical system by a simpler one, the "model" made up of a finite number of particles, at most a few hundred. The behaviour of the model is predicted by means of a powerful computer which determines the evolution of a large number of configurations starting from a large number of initial configurations. It is sometimes claimed that more than a theoretical study, simulation is an experiment where the experimental equipment is the computer.

A radical trend in that direction is the position of one of the most brilliant representatives of modern theoretical physics. He claims that the key to the unsolved theoretical problems facing physics nowadays is the computer. In order to progress toward the solution, the most urgent task is therefore to make better computers specially designed for specific purposes, a task to which the theorists should devote their best efforts. My personal reaction to this idea is the same as that of the good wife of Bishop Wilberforce upon learning that according to Sir Charles Darwin, Man descended from the ape. "If this horrible piece of news turns out to be true, lets's pray to God that it does not get around."

What Use is Physics?*

What use is physics? When a profession begins to question itself in this way it has reached crisis point.

Our first problem is the lack of money and in the long run it may prove fatal. I shall not bore you with statistics, everyone involved, government ministries, the DGRST (Direction Générale de la Recherche Scientifique et Technique), the CNRS (Centre National de la Recherche Scientifique) and the CEA (Commissariat à l'Énergie Atomique), each has figures of its own and each has its own method of defining research, capital expenditure, operating costs, and cash flow. Two things are certain. In our country the fraction of the gross national product spent on research is continally decreasing at a rate which, for the last three years, exceeds 10% per annum. Furthermore, the number of appointments and openings for young research scientists is steadily falling and poses a worrisome problem in the short term and an agonising one in the long term. At the same time we are undergoing a painful reappraisal of science and particularly of physics. It has taken on the nature of a confrontation, to use a word very much in fashion these days.

The criticism comes from port and starboard. On the one side the complaint is that physics does not provide value for money, that it does not make a big enough contribution to the things that really matter for modern civilization and the well-being of mankind—cars, dishwashers, colour television, intercontinental missiles and hydrogen bombs. From the other

* Centenary conference of the French Physical Society, held at Vittel, 28 May-2 June, 1973.

89

side comes the opposite reproach that physics has been too successful in these despicable goals.

There is yet another group that argues that physics has achieved practically all its objectives, that there is nothing very interesting left to do and that the time has come to move on to other areas such as biology, medicine and "human" sciences, the only ones likely to bring happiness to our society, subjects which the Americans, with little respect, call the "soft" sciences.

Finally there is the tendency, usually directed against science in general rather than physics in particular, but where physics is the prime target because it is the "hardest" of sciences in the sense defined above, to deplore the abuses of scientific knowledge which are in conflict with our intuition and instinct.

I shall try to answer these accusations later. I would simply say that this is a case of applying the sentence, that is to say cutting off the funds for physics, before the trial has been held. As the Queen said, in Alice in Wonderland, "Sentence first, verdict afterwards."

First of all the physicists. What are their reasons for choosing physics? The prime reason, and there is no need to feel ashamed of it, is that it is their job and their livelihood. Long and difficult study is needed in preparation for it and not everyone is cut out for that, far from it, so physicists can hardly be accused of choosing their profession because they are not equipped to do anything else. I choose my words with care when I say that the vast majority of physicists are men and women who work harder and who are more gifted than the average university student. Since they are too few to form a pressure group, and since their voting strength is negligible, must we compel them to choose between begging for a living and revolt?

The second reason for choosing physics is that they enjoy it, the scoundrels.

I shall be careful not to suggest any parallel between holding forth on the subject of science compared with actually doing it, and holding forth on the subject of love... Nevertheless although the day-to-day life of the physicist is made up mostly of dreary tasks often without great interest, I think that more than once in our careers we have all derived from our work some satisfaction which helps to make life seem worth living after all. It is not always a case of a personal achievement, it might be that, after poring over someone's apparently obscure theory, the penny finally drops—rather like the image seen through binoculars which all at once comes into focus revealing its true meaning and full beauty. It might also be the experience of hearing for the first time about a simple, elegant and crucial experiment. How much more satisfying when it is a question of an original discovery (even a minor one) something that no-one else in the world has ever seen before you.

Those who have never had such an experience have perhaps made the wrong decision in choosing a physicist's career.

Finally, there is a third reason for studying physics—the satisfaction of performing a task essential to mankind. I use the word mankind, as opposed to society, quite deliberately because I feel that the latter is ambiguous.

It is important now to examine the basic aims of physics. This need not take much space, we all know what it is about.

Physics teaches us understanding of the material world in which we live and the laws which govern it. It seems to me that for man, as a thinking being, there may be tasks more immediately urgent but none more important.

Thought is not man's sole activity, the brain is not everything and it has other functions besides scientific investigation. Nevertheless, do what we will, we shall never be as strong as a horse, as affectionate as a dog or as passionate as a baboon.

If man's existence is ever to amount to anything more than a minor digression in the evolution of life on our planet, if we are something more than a mollusc, a rat or a cow, the difference must lie in a rational intelligence, and science is one of the purest examples of this.

If to hold such beliefs is tantamount to that dangerous aberration which some call scientism then, fine! I am one of them.

To understand the material world is to master it, to escape the tyranny of the forces of nature.

Today it has become fashionable to present nature as infinitely bountiful, the Earth-Mother, hurt and disfigured by her ungrateful children; we too easily forget the hardship and terror she inflicted upon us before we learned how to unlock her secrets.

There is no use denying that modern technology, born out of our conquests in the fields of physics (and chemistry) carries with it a train of dangers and evils. But does it follow that the physicist, whose *fundamental* discoveries made possible some new technology misused by society, is any more to be blamed than anyone else? Should he submit his discoveries to autocriticism—or, better still, to a tribunal of his own colleagues—should there be an "Order' of physicists, guardian of the ethics of the profession?

However that may be, it seems to me that the balance sheet for technology generated by physics is still well in the black. This state of affairs may be reversed in times to come if we are not careful, but that is a problem for society as a whole, a *political* problem. The most that physicists can do is to help formulate the problem to the extent that they are better informed about some aspects of the question (which is not always the case); they cannot, and I go as far as to say, should not, impose *their* solution on the community.

In any case there is no going back. We shall never again see the good farm labourer trudging behind his two brown-and-white oxen fourteen hours a day. Nor shall we see his wife doing her washing by the river, rain or shine, mother of twelve children of whom all but two died in infancy; nor the beautiful Puy lace and lace-workers blind by the age of fifteen, nor the fine meat of the old days without hormones or additives, which half the population saw but once a year. This idyll will never return; the noble savage is a thing of the past.

I have called to mind two important aspects of physics that can be summarized thus: fundamental research to achieve some understanding of the world in which we live, applied research to acquire mastery over it. In one as in the other, physics is not unique; other sciences such as chemistry, geology, meteorology, the life sciences, medicine, agronomy and doubtless many others play an essential role.

Physics, as we said before, is a "hard" science, the keystone of the whole edifice.

For example, what would happen in the life sciences if they had to do without the tools provided by physics: X-rays, electron microscopes, the ultracentrifuge, spectrometers, radio isotopes, radiation counters and all the apparatus of medical electronics...

This logistic support of other sciences by physics, important though it may be, is not the only service, nor perhaps the most essential. If molecular biology has made lightning progress it is due in large part to the use of the concepts and methodology of physics.

Thus, in a certain sense, physics provides the other sciences with the necessary hardware—and software too.

So far we have treated physics, the tool of pure and applied research, in terms of the science itself and the support it provides for the other sciences. It remains to say a few words about physics in the context of secondary and further education. There too, we can identify two aspects.

The study of physics is a cultural discipline on an equal footing with poetry, history, philosophy or the so-called modern mathematics. Whatever career a pupil or student has in mind, he will derive from physics an understanding of the world and an intellectual challenge quite on a par with those provided by Shakespeare's sonnets, the battle of Hastings, deductive logic, or Euclidean geometry.

The other educational aspect of physics is the influence it has on a wide spectrum of scientific and technical activities. This is self-evident for engineers and chemists, and each day becomes more and more applicable to a multitude of professions—medicine, architecture, agronomy, aviation, etc.

I would now like to return to the assertion that the entire edifice of physical knowledge is now virtually complete, that all the principal discoveries have been made, and that, though there may be a few more details to clear up, the time has now come to move on to other fields that are newer and more exciting, such as the life sciences or the social sciences.

Personally I find the physics I do just as challenging and fascinating as it always was, and if the problems sometimes appear to be more difficult, or the solutions suggested by my young colleagues more complicated than before, this is merely one of those unfortunate signs of our times, like steeper stairs and smaller newsprint.

Need I remind you that it was towards the end of the last century when minds as distinguished as Mach and Poincaré were proclaiming that the classical edifice of physics was essentially complete—just at the time when the extraordinary revolution of relativity and the quantum theory was about to bring the whole thing tumbling down. And we can scarcely avoid mention of the assertion of that great experimentalist Albert Michelson, "We have now reached the stage where there is nothing left to measure but the sixth decimal place", that very sixth decimal place which, in his own famous experiment, laid waste the proud palace of absolute space and time.

At this precise moment (1973), following an appreciable period in the doldrums, physics is taking off again in an extraordinary fashion. From infinitely small to infinitely large, from elementary particles to the structure of the universe, through condensed matter in all its forms, all is in flux, both theory and experiment. The time of the summing up has not yet come. There are more things in Heaven and Earth than are dreamed of in your philosophy, and as another Englishman, the writer Aldous Huxley, said "There is still no salt on the tail of the Almighty".

Another thing. In his beautiful book, *Chance and Necessity*, Jacques Monod lays the foundation for ethics and morals based on scientific thought. My own ideas about such problems are a long way from being such a coherent and ambitious design—they are more like feelings than ideas—but they border on certain themes advanced by Monod.

One of the marks of modern life is that lying is everywhere. (Perhaps this was always the case and it is just more visible today.) Everyone lies—politicians in power, of course, but also those who aspire to replace them, the news media and the demonstrators, left-wing and right-wing, diplomats and technocrats, demagogues and pedagogues. Crimes against humanity, past and present, are certain to be first of all explained, then justified and finally glorified as history is written.

Don't misunderstand me. I do not say that none of this matters, that it is six of one and half-a-dozen of the other. If it is deplorable to falsify the truth to defend an unjust cause, it might be acceptable in order to defend the oppressed, the weak, or the innocent. I make no judgement, what right have I? I simply make a statement of fact. If so many young men and women today are disturbed, lost, alienated or simply cynical, I think it is because of the lying we see spreading everywhere. Scientists, of course, are no exception. The professor who puts his name on publications to which he has made no contribution is perpetrating a lie. Someone who sits on all the committees and the boards of directors and then complains bitterly that he has no time for research, someone who has already built his career but criticises the young scientists for lack of dedication and idealism, these are all liars. So too are those who flatter the young, applaud everything they do, however absurd, in an attempt to follow the trend.

Liars too some young turks of the universities, dons and half-dons, whose names are well known and the scientific publication well-hidden. They use rhetoric and violence as a smokescreen to hide their unbridled ambition, their laziness, or their jealousy towards their colleagues who are more talented or more successful.

What is this leading up to? For my argument to be complete, all you would need to do would be to prove that I too am a liar, by exposing my hidden motives for writing these last paragraphs.

What I mean to say is that there is one area where the scientist—for us, the physicist—does not lie, that is in his scientific publications, otherwise he is found out sooner or later.

Lavoisier held the post of *fermier général** that is to say a man who gets rich at the expense of the common people, Cauchy was a terrible right-wing reactionary, Stark was a Nazi, but their scientific work was *true*. In our own day, certain attitudes adopted by such-and-such scientist might seem to be prompted by paranoia, but his article on time-reversal is immortal.

Pilate asked "What is truth?" Well we can give him an answer, "Here is truth of a kind".

Is this enough to form the basis of a code of morals, or to guide our consciences? Certainly not. Nevertheless in the marshy ground of the modern world, giving way under our feet, where even the best of men are sometimes beset by despair or cynicism, it's good to have some firm ground to stand on, a truth. That, to my mind, is a further justification for science, in our case, physics.

There is a problem I do not wish to sidestep, and that is that of the physicist who is involved in military matters. Professor Casimir, President of the European Physical Society, gave a conference in Wiesbaden in

---

* A sort of Crown Agent responsible for the King's lands.

October 1972 entitled "Physics and Society" where he made this recommendation: "It is my personal opinion that, in view of the alarming uses of science-based technology in warfare no scientist in an academic position should, of his own free will, be active or advise on military technology. As I said, this is a personal opinion, but I know that it is shared by many of my colleagues and an impressive number of students".

Note Casimir's recommendation carries the qualification "at the present time".

I am honoured to count among my friends some English physicists who have worked on military problems, radar in fact, not only in time of war, but in peace time from 1937-1939, having academic appointments at the same time. Personally I think they were right, and that they helped save England from the Nazis, and I would have done the same in their place.

It seems to me that to work, or to refrain from working on military projects is not a question of some universal code of professional ethics of the physicist. For each physicist, each separate case is a problem for his individual conscience, and a political question. If I greatly deplore the fact that a great scientist, whose genius I admire, Murray Gell-Mann, consented to join the famous Jason committee, that is because that committee was advising the government on the conduct of a war of aggression that was unjust, cruel and absurd. (Written in 1973).

It is time to conclude. I have tried to show why, to my mind, physics is both beautiful and useful, and why we must continue to study it. I don't know whether I have convinced you, nor do I know whether this audience is the one that it is most urgent to convince. Perhaps it is though, and this is the reason.

At the same time that resources are being cut and career opportunities restricted, there has been a concerted campaign to belittle this discipline and make the physicist ashamed of his profession.

They are accused of being useless spendthrift parasites. They are told that the man-in-the-street cannot understand the need for their expensive toys—the radiotelescopes or the accelerators—and it is about time they began to explain to him what purpose these machines actually serve.

Exaggerated respect for the man-in-the-street, who has never been told the reason for selling 200,000 tons of butter at two francs the kilogram while the housewife pays eight francs, nor the reason for building the abattoirs at la Villette, which no-one wants, at a price comparable to that of the accelerator at CERN!

Physicists are told that if they are to be tolerated at all, they should give up their pointless games with elementary particles, superfluids or pulsars, in order to devote themselves to the problems of pollution, the environment and urban decay, and more generally, all the tasks that society has in mind for them. Physics has failed; physics has been a disappointment; physics should be made to pay for its mistakes.

There is an old French proverb, "If you want to drown your dog, say it has rabies". In all the industrialized nations, faced with the burden of unproductive spending, which in the United States in particular has reached monstrous proportions, faced with the pressures to remedy social inequalities, governments tighten belts and cut back wherever they can if they see that there will be no disastrous short-term consequences or that there is no social backlash to be feared.

Physicists are not perfect, far from it. They have, for sure, wasted money either on research of doubtful utility, or on interesting research carried out with too little intelligent planning. No doubt much could be said on the right way to organize research and how this control could be optimized, but that is a different debate. I nevertheless believe, in all conscience, that the balance sheet of physics (not, I emphasize, the senseless uses to which society sometimes puts it) is positive. I believe that the physicists have not let us down and that, as long as they do good research, they can have a clear conscience.

On Fundamental Research*

My attitude towards fundamental research is the same as that expressed by a colleague of an Academy from a different discipline with regard to the concept of virtue—"It deserves to be encouraged". The next step is to find a precise definition of the object of this encouragement.

What then is fundamental research? Above all, what distinguishes it from its cousin, applied research? Consciously or unwittingly, in the press or in speeches the two are often mixed up, which is harmless, but when this confusion extends to the provision of resources and financial support it could be more dangerous.

Fundamental research, applied research, it is easy to make the mistake — scientists with the same training use similar or even identical equipment in the same type of laboratory to conduct experiments which look the same and may even be the same; where then is the difference? There is one and it is crucial. It consists in the choice of problem and the frame of mind with which it is tackled.

I hope I can be forgiven for choosing examples all from the field of physics. A certain distaste for talking about a subject of which one knows very little is merely the self-indulgence of the pure scientist.

In fundamental research, the aim is to understand the laws of nature: the phenomenon under investigation should be as simple and as general as possible.

For example, in solid-state physics (where the distinction between

* Opening session of the *Académie des Sciences*, 7 January 1980.

99

pure and applied research is least clear) one would choose to work with a sample of high purity (chemical or even isotopic), with a simple, well-understood, crystalline structure, and perhaps of a simple geometrical shape if surface effects could be important. Having removed as many of the inessential complicating factors as possible, we expect to be able to obtain a complete understanding of the phenomenon.

Objections could be made to the effect that recent solid state investigations have used amorphous disordered materials, often full of defects and impurities. Do not be deceived by this. Although it may be true that initially there were immediate or potential practical applications, in the end this very disorder turns out to be as simple, as general and in the final analysis as "clean" as the perfectly ordered structures mentioned above. *"Ce beau désordre est un effet de l'art."*

In applied research the goal is to obtain a device which works and which is useful; it may be an advantage (and rewarding) to understand everything that is going on, but that is by no means essential.

The applied scientist might say, "If it works, I do not care why", whereas the pure scientist might say "I do not care if it doesn't work, as long as I know why."

In applied research, the choice of the sample material may well be dictated by economic and technical factors, often incompatible with the desire for a simple structure that would provide a better understanding of the underlying phenomena. I would like to give an example, now rather out-of-date, from the time when France was studying the graphite-gas method for nuclear reactors. (This was before it was accepted that nuclear energy was right-wing, reactionary and imperialist, while oil was left-wing, revolutionary and liberating.)

In the technology of this graphite-gas method, it was essential to discover the effect of nuclear radiation on artificial graphite, a complex, poorly-characterized material, used as a neutron moderator. For the purposes of a fundamental investigation of the effects of radiation, a single crystal of silicon would have been a much better choice, but it is unsuitable as a moderator because it does not slow down the neutrons effectively enough and it would be far too costly. It turned out however that the semiconductor industry was quite interested in the problem of neutron irradiation of single crystals of silicon and, lo and behold, fundamental research became applied research again.

Long ago when I was still at my high-school desk, when all my teachers still had degrees and polo-neck sweaters had not yet replaced their starched collars, when jeans had yet to take over from their striped trousers, in this distant past I was taught the key to classical tragedy: the reason why we only find characters of high rank — kings, princesses — an explanation on a high intellectual, not to say scientific, plane. The point was that feelings of hate, love, jealousy and pity are then expressed in all their purity and strength; they may be better examined and understood when separated from minor complications such as the need to earn a living by ploughing the fields or going to the office.

In this sense fundamental research is classical tragedy while applied research is middle-class drama or the situation-comedy; in these, the day-to-day routine does not leave the characters time to express their feelings in the pure state.

The interactions between mathematicians and physicists, not always smooth, provide an insight into some aspects of the dichotomy between pure and applied research.

This difference of approach was neatly expressed by a great contemporary physicist and Nobel laureate, Felix Bloch, with whom I once had the privilege of working. "Take your problem to a mathematician", he said, "and he will explain that it is incorrectly formulated and will redefine it for you. When this is done he will then prove that the problem has no solution, and will be surprised that you are not pleased with this result".

I remember a conversation with a mathematician, some time ago, during which I tried to interest him in certain important unsolved problems associated with phase transitions. Having overcome the language barrier, I was able to convince him that it was basically a problem in pure mathematics. I found his reply particularly enlightening, "I appreciate that this problem might interest the physicists, but for mathematicians like us, this problem, and more generally, this type of problem, suffers from two fatal flaws: first it is far too specialized and has no wider application; its eventual solution is of no interest to me, in my chosen field of mathematics;

secondly and above all, it is an extremely difficult problem and I cannot be sure of solving it." I was not too happy with this reply, and then I began to think back... I remembered that several months ago my coworkers were approached by the Department of Fast Neutrons of the French Atomic Energy Commission (CEA): under bombardment by fast neutrons, the stainless steel casings of the fuel elements were deformed and warped; wouldn't it be possible to undertake an investigation of a fundamental nature in order to try to understand this phenomenon and describe these deformations quantitatively? I remember my reaction, "These fuel rods have a complex geometry, the neutron spectrum is not known with any certainty, the composition of the stainless steel varies from one batch of rods to the next: it is too specialized a problem and too difficult to be of interest to us", the very same reply that the mathematician had given to the problem I had outlined to him.

I should add that some of these problems were later solved by theoretical physicists. The principal reason for their success hinges on the fact that they chose the problem themselves and had their hearts in it, rather than having a problem imposed on them from outside.

I hope that these few examples—there are many others that could be cited—have shown that the qualification "fundamental" or "applied" for a piece of research is a function of the state of mind of the scientist involved. This quite naturally leads me to the question of the personality, education and career of the pure scientist.

To my mind the first requirement of a pure scientist is talent. I shall not try to define what that means. After all, when we speak of the talent of a singer, a musician, a composer, a writer, a painter, a sculptor or a comedian, do we feel a need to explain what it means? If we make less mention of the talent of a tax inspector, a judge, a solicitor, a lorry driver or a Minister of Parliament, this should not be interpreted to mean that the intellectual, physical or moral qualities required by these honourable occupations on some suitable scale of values, are in any way inferior to those of the "talented" professions mentioned above. In my opinion talent is characterized by its specificity. The person who becomes a judge, in other circumstances might well have made a success as a solicitor, tax collector, minister or even lorry driver. I think this is not true for the singer or the comedian, and it is not true for the scientific researcher. *Poeta nascitur non fit*. I hasten to add that the scientist should find no reason to boast about this peculiarity of his chosen profession and think of himself as the salt of the earth. In our times the basketball player has no chance of success unless he is at least 6 feet 8 inches tall. He should not look down (figuratively) on other mortals who are only 5 feet 8 inches tall.

How can a scientist be sure that he has not made a mistake in choosing this career? I have borrowed the answer from Abbé Jérome Coignard, the "human scientist" described by Anatole France. "Abbé, why translate Zozime?" asks Monsieur d'Anquetil. "If you want to know the truth' he replied "I feel some sensuality in the act". Now sensuality is a big word. Nevertheless, if the scientist's everyday life is made up of tasks without any great sparkle or even challenge, I believe that each has known some time in his professional life, and more than once, that satisfaction which helps to convince him that life is worth living after all. How strong is that reward when it represents the discovery of a new result, even one of minor importance! This feeling of having done or seen something never done or seen before by anyone else in the world! Those who have never had such an experience have been misled in choosing the career of research scientist. And in parallel with the joy of discovery, one finds inescapably the agonies of the scientist, the agonies of the fruitless search. And there too, I would have little time for a scientist who had not experienced such setbacks. More frequent and more of a torment for the theoretician with his blank sheet of paper, than for the experimentalist, who even in the absence of inspiration usually finds something to tinker with in his laboratory, this agony may sometimes become traumatic and the scientist reaches breaking point. Some look for escape into politics or the trade unions where they tend to take extremist positions, others move into administrative or managerial positions with an exalted sense of their own importance. A happier solution is to have some teaching responsibilities as well as the research. By throwing themselves into these teaching duties these scientists can maintain their self-esteem and self-respect without which existence becomes intolerable, while they wait for the inspiration or the lucky break which will allow their research to get started once more.

I have said enough to show that the education and selection of young people for careers in research is both important and tricky. Are our own methods suitable? I doubt it. In a remarkably clear and forceful analysis of the teaching of mathematics in France, Paul Germain extended his remarks to the whole of our scientific education. He quoted figures which give cause for concern: since the war there have been a hundred Nobel laureates from the U.S.A., thirty from Britain and five from France. One is tempted to ask, "What is it that we lack?" Some might turn the question around and enquire maliciously, "What is it that we have and they lack? Could it be the *Grandes Écoles*, so envied by the rest of the world?"

If we exclude the biological and medical sciences all our scientific elite come from the *Grandes Écoles*. As an example, of the seven top physicists elected to the French Academy of Science since its reformation, only one was not from a *Grande École*, and he was born abroad and only came to France as an adult. Critics might suggest that the *Grandes Écoles* are merely a Spanish inn where you only find what you bring with you *. Perhaps those who come out are only the best (which is not in dispute) because those that got in were the best. And are those best, bettered while still in? Is all for the best in the best of worlds? Other critics (or perhaps the same ones) might point out another peculiarity of the French system which is the envy of the world, the recent reorganization of our Universities. *Grande École* and University, the cream and the skimmed milk: why not use whole milk? We shall leave the devil's advocate to answer his own questions.

Advancement in a scientific career naturally depends on the value of the scientific work, but the procedure for evaluating this is by no means straightforward. Coworkers and research directors are of course in the best position to judge, but can we depend on their judgement? Would it be completely impartial?

The accepted criterion for judging a scientist or a laboratory is the quality and volume of their scientific publications. This practice, which in theory is perfectly reasonable, unfortunately leads to a diversion of the system of scientific publications from its goal which is the reporting of

---

* A French saying.

knowledge, an essential requirement for progress in research. Unfortunately it is much easier to measure volume than quality. The result is a veritable explosion of publications where the numbers exceed all reasonable limits. An American colleague told me recently, "What can you do, money is now so tight, you have to publish twice as much to get the same amount of support." The trouble is, the number of *good* publications hardly increases at all.

Our American colleagues have invented a scheme designed to circumvent these difficulties, the famous "Science Citation Index" which uses computer methods to assess the work of a particular scientist according to the number of times his publications have been cited in the literature within a given period of time. Unfortunately this sophisticated technique is scarcely more reliable than the primitive method based on counting the number of publications and the number of pages in each.

Of course it is easy to detect the obvious trick of citing one's own work. It is more difficult to unmask a "ring" where A cites B, B cites C and C cites A, but no doubt the computer could be programmed to check for such conspiracies too. Several years ago it happened that I wrote an article which contained an error in the calculation. A colleague pointed this out and continues to point it out in his own publications with some regularity. Each time the computer, that faithful hound, adds another citation to the index on my account, raising my international standing. I persist in the belief that the old-fashioned method of actually reading the publications is both safer and surer. However it must be possible to relieve the pressure for publication, leaving the scientist free to pursue his career and publish only when he really has something new to say. Quality would be enhanced, quantity diminished, a double advantage.

It is scarcely any easier to assess the performance of a laboratory on financial criteria. When it was my job to take care of such matters, one swore by the "cost per scientist" the ratio of the laboratory budget (excepting salaries) to the number of research workers involved, which quite often led to the inclusion in the calculation of personnel only distantly related to research work, just to keep the unit cost down. In particular, one came to the surprising conclusion that it was more efficient to attack a given scientific problem with ten men rather than with five.

The question of the usefulness of older scientists is a matter of controversy. It is easy to say that research is for young people, and that above a certain age inventiveness dries up and it is better to call it a day. In support of this view, one may quote a long list of examples of important discoveries made by young men. Although I cannot claim to be entirely impartial in this matter, I do believe that the idea stems from a mistaken analysis and a confusion between two quite different qualities: genius and talent.

I shall not try to define genius any more than I defined talent. Infinitely more rare than talent, genius is distinguished by two features: in the scientist at least it makes its appearance much earlier in life and unfortunately often, if not always, disappears earlier too. Examples of great discoveries made in early life which we are so pleased to cite, are the work of the genius. Their enormous importance in the field of discovery should not blind us to the fact that, in number, they are statistically negligible and need not be taken into account when determining research policy. I believe that the talented scientist (I pointed out earlier that these alone should undertake a scientific career) retains his intellectual capacities for investigation and discovery to the end of his career, short of an accident.

However the talented scientist does run the risk of losing with age his enthusiasm, his sense of wonder when faced with a new discovery: when one can look back on five or six discoveries (not of major importance, that would be for the genius) it is not so evident that a seventh is worth all the time and trouble. And, even if you are not slipping back it is hard to accept the idea that you are not making some actual progress, to recognize that you have reached your peak: this is the real reason why so many scientists of talent make their escape into the higher grades of management and administration, into, to be frank, their untimely demise as a scientist.

It is important, even essential, that the administration of science is carried on by those who have first-hand experience of creative science; it is a pity that in France so much talent gets bogged down in it. Perhaps a better solution would be to take on such administrative duties earlier in life so as to be able to get out again before it is too late.

We all accept that science and technology will be expected to solve the immense problems confronting our society. In the field of applied science this involves an enormous effort in analysis, planning, organization and above all financial support, for "Science without money can be soul-destroying" (*Science sans finance n'est que ruine de l'âme*) *. I confess I have some reservations about all that planning. Nowadays we hear much of the catch phrase "Piloting of research from downstream" but I remain unconvinced. My reservations are not motivated by some abstract concept of scientific freedom nor by the ridiculous prejudice that applied research is any less noble than fundamental research; I do not mind getting my hands dirty. No, my concern is for the effectiveness of the operation. I do not believe in mixing the two kinds of research. *Age quod agis.* All too often in my career I have seen mediocre work justified by the authors on the grounds that it might eventually prove useful, thereby hoping to excuse its lack of precision and rigour, or justified on the grounds of its fundamental interest, thinking to excuse its obvious impracticality. In my opinion "downstream" is not the place to control fundamental research. The end-user should be aware of his needs, his outlets, his medium and long-term markets, and having weighed them all up he can then ask what it is he expects from research according to some suitable agreed procedure. This applied research is, I repeat, just as noble and fascinating as pure science, but it should be recognized for exactly what it is. In order to make reasonable demands on research, the end-user needs to know what is possible and feasible in practice in the present state of the art of research. It is a question of organization. Moreover he should pay for what he requires. There again, not for reasons of ideology but because it is the only way to ensure that he knows what he wants and that his requests are well thought out.

As for fundamental research, it should not let itself be bothered with what happens downstream. Pure science is the goose that lays the golden eggs, often quite capriciously. That unfortunately is her nature. We should be very careful not to kill her by being in too much of a hurry.

---

* "Science sans *conscience* n'est que ruine de l'âme" is what Rabelais said.

The Use of French
in Scientific Communication*

> ... *cette honorable universalité de la langue française si*
> *bien reconnue et hautement avouée dans notre Europe.*
> Rivarol (1784)
> *The English tongue is of small reach stretching no further*
> *than this island of ours.*   Richard Mulcaster (1582)

The use of the French language in scientific communications presents a delicate problem because there are two conflicting requirements. Let us try to formulate the problem properly and dispassionately. It is understood that the present discussion applies only to fundamental research. Applied research and development have their own particular problems which could lead to different conclusions.

Let me point out certain basic truths in the simplest possible terms. There is no science without communication; what cannot be communicated to others is not scientific. To do science, each of us must know what others are doing at home and abroad, particularly abroad, not because their science is better but because of the scale, which is no doubt ten or twenty times larger. We must therefore understand what the rest of the world is communicating to us, by the written and spoken word.

We must also communicate our own results abroad. It is important to understand why this is an equally crucial requirement. In exchange for the information we have received? Of course. As a contribution to the image of

* Bulletin of the French Physical Society, July 1982.

France seen from abroad? Certainly. But the real reason lies elsewhere. Our scientific work needs to be examined, criticised and tested abroad, compared with results obtained elsewhere that are sometimes in conflict and sometimes complementary. Without such comparisons and the international competition that is aroused by them, our own science would wither, become parochial, perhaps go astray and in the final analysis waste away in a fairly short time. In the domain of pure science, our much-prized national independence is neither possible nor desirable.

Whatever the numerous and varied motivations that drive a scientist to publish his work, we are forced in the end to publish abroad, not through altruism, nor for the prestige of our contry, however noble these causes, but because the vitality of French science is at stake. By generally raising the standard of French science such publications contribute indirectly in the long term to the prestige and renown of France.

If we accept the premise of the overriding importance of understanding what is said and written abroad and of communicating our own scientific work to the outside world, we should take a close look at this world of science today before trying to decide how and whether to change it.

At the present time it is no exaggeration to say that the international language of science is English, or at least the English spoken and written not only by the British and Americans, but also, with mixed success, by the representatives of all the developed countries, Japanese and Scandinavians, Germans and Dutch, French, Italians and Spaniards, Belgians and Israelis, Russians and East Europeans. With the exception of these last two groups, the vast majority of national scientific journals, reviews and specialist monographs tend to adopt English to a greater and greater extent. English is also the scientific language of the great developing nations, India, Pakistan, Latin America and the Arab countries apart from North Africa.

This has become the common working language of the scientists, their *lingua franca*. The anglo-saxons sometimes say "The true language of science is broken English". For brevity I shall call it henceforth *"anglo-*
pük", a contraction of English and Volapük. The inverse would be what

Etiemble calls "Atlantic French" or *franglais* which according to him is French contaminated with Greek by the pedants, with English by the snobs and with American by big business. In the case of *anglopük* the victim is Shakespeare rather than Racine.

The role of this common language today is comparable with that of the Latin used by the scientists of the seventeenth and eighteenth centuries. (It is quite possible that our English would have horrified Newton, but then what would Cicero and Tacitus have thought of the Latin used in Newton's *Principia?*)

This overriding need to communicate, mentioned earlier, explains why the representatives of great civilizations like Germany or Italy, whose languages are perfectly capable of expressing all the subtleties of scientific thought, have accepted *anglopük* as a means of communication without any particular reservations.

Moreover *anglopük* is an easy language compared with literary and poetic English, with only a rudimentary vocabulary and very simple grammar. This is not the least of its attractions as an everyday means of communication.

Are our young scientists handicapped by the widespread use of *anglopük*, compared with their English-speaking colleagues? Doubtless they are, but much less than some of their older colleagues. The teaching of modern languages, and in particular English, has improved considerably during the last decade or two. Audiovisual techniques, visits abroad, contacts with foreign visitors, magazines and text-books in English, all help the young people of today much more than the older generation.

If their English composition leaves something to be desired, it must be admitted that standards of writing have fallen everywhere, France included, to such an extent that they write scarcely any better in French, and their Anglo-American colleagues write equally poor English. The English-speakers, using their mother-tongue, do have a marked advantage in the oral discussions which follow the lectures at a scientific conference, but this advantage should not be overestimated. A scientific discussion is not a test of eloquence, and the one who is fundamentally right usually manages to win the argument. Paradoxically, it may be the young English-speakers that are more handicapped by the general use of *anglopük*. Over and above the irritation of seeing their mother-tongue mutilated, the lack of incentive for learning a foreign language may in the end turn out to be a considerable cultural loss. In contrast, by being forced to learn English, the young French scientist has the key to understanding English and American civilization, their theatre, their cinema, their customs and (why not?) their literature, history and poetry.

The parallel between *anglopük*, the everyday language of these times, and Latin, the common language of three centuries ago, is not exact. The Latin of the seventeenth century was a dead language. *Anglopük* is a bastardized version of the language used by several active nations and in particular the most powerful nation in the world, the United States. This is not surprising: French, too, was the international language at the time that France was the most populous and powerful nation of Europe.

Can we, and should we forbid the use of *anglopük* for this reason, as many have demanded from time to time over the years? If so, what would replace it? The answer to the second question is easy; since Latin is quite dead and Esperanto still-born, we would use French exclusively for all transactions with foreign scientists. What would happen then? Three scenarios are possible:

(a) Favourably impressed, all other countries adopt French as the vehicle of communication. A seductive idea, but unlikely.

(b) The nations which do not speak English, convinced by our example, decide to express themselves in their own languages. The result—the tower of Babel; besides English we would have to learn all the foreign languages mentioned above. A nuisance, but also unlikely.

(c) The other nations do not follow our example, which is the only realistic assumption. The result—we still have to master *anglopük* in order to understand the others. As for ourselves we should be understood by Québécois, Acadians, Walloons, French-speaking Swiss, Haitians and some French-speaking Africans. While this might be eminently desirable, is it really good enough in today's world to ensure full exposure to the science of the outside world, which we said was so badly needed?

It seems to follow from what has just been said that *anglopük* offers an acceptable solution to the problem of communicating with foreign scientists.

Things are not as simple as that; if *anglopük* is used uncritically, in the long run it constitutes certain dangers to the survival of French as a means of scientific communication. These dangers are not as serious or as insurmountable as it was sometimes claimed. However, they must be clearly recognized and guarded against.

The first danger is the corruption of our language by misuse of terminology and turns of phrase derived from scientific English. This is what Etiemble has denounced as "Atlantic French" or *"franglais"*, which differs from useful *anglopük*, in being the poisoned fruit of our laziness and negligence. For years now, many have denounced its depredations, either with amusement or indignation, according to temperament.

Such punctures in the fabric of our language must be taken seriously but not as a tragedy. We must all take pains to avoid such damage and make sure others do likewise. On the other hand we should not be carried away by an excess of zeal in our defence of the language against outside influences. Some foreign words have been given freedom of the city — no-one would think of using *moment cinétique intrinsèque* instead of spin, or of inventing a translation for quark. It would perhaps be as well to remember that in science, as in geography in earlier times, the privilege of choosing the name falls to the discoverer.

The second danger, which is more serious, is that as a result of not publishing in their native language and of speaking only *anglopük* in international conferences, French scientists reach the point of not being able to use their own language as a means of scientific expression.

There are still, thank God, some effective safety-nets. Our university education, our graduate courses and our tutorials are all conducted in French. Similarly our examinations are written in French, as are diplomas, master's and doctor's theses (although here the option of presenting part of the work in the form of articles published in English is the thin end of a wedge which should be carefully watched). There are many national conferences, on general or specialized topics, organized by our scientific societies; these are very successful and provide numerous opportunities for our research workers to express themselves in French.

A particular effort must be made on behalf of French-speaking foreigners who are struggling to retain their cultural identity under difficult conditions. It would be a good idea to set up the machinery to ensure that they receive regular invitations to our national scientific conferences. Financial support should come from the budget of External Affairs rather than Research.

Finally the Academy of Science has a fundamental role to play in this matter. The published reports, kept up-to-date by the efforts of the permanent Secretaries with the help of many of our colleagues, reach an ever-growing audience that could only increase still further if the articles were accompanied by a comprehensive abstract in English.

Remember that all the French scientific journals (that goes without saying) but also all the international journals with the European label accept articles written in the French language. It would be dangerous to allow this right (this *easement* in legal terminology) to fall into disuse. In order to safeguard our position and keep our options open for the future, it would be wise to maintain a continuous flow of publications in French, even if moderate in volume. This task should fall principally upon well-established scientists with a solid reputation abroad, who are still working at full capacity. They would have the sometimes thankless task of keeping the sea-lanes open through the encroaching ice of *anglopük*. However if a French scientist decides to publish in English for the justifiable reason that this guarantees a wider dissemination of the work, his freedom of choice should be respected, for science cannot flourish without freedom. In the same way, it would be inadmissible in an international conference organized in France that a participant were not permitted to express himself in French. Nevertheless, if English is also an official language of the conference, and if he decides to present his work in this language in order to be more widely understood, then here too his choice should be respected, whatever his nationality. It is undesirable that the rules governing oral presentations in an international scientific meeting should depend on the nationality of the speaker. Such an arrangement would only be misunderstood by scientists from abroad and would create an undesirable image of our country in the eyes of the rest of the world.

Apart from oral or written scientific communications of whatever length, which have been discussed above, there is another arena open to French-speaking scientists which has been insufficiently exploited. There are three types of work: university textbooks, popular science books and articles, and specialist textbooks or monographs. In contrast to the day-to-day publications in scientific journals, where information content takes precedence over style, and which tolerate *anglopük* reasonably well, the publications mentioned above give the French-speaking scientist free rein to exploit the clarity and stylistic qualities of his native tongue.

For the first two types of publication, the French scientific market is large enough to make it profitable for high-quality writing. French publishers (who have not always acted for the best in these matters) would simply have to ensure that they obtained the best advice on seeking out authors that are well-qualified educationally and scientifically. They should also be more selective in deciding to translate foreign publications into French, for these have often been slap-dash translations of mediocre material.

Specialist textbooks and monographs present a particular problem since the French scientific market may be too narrow to make this kind of work an economic proposition. Consequently, publication in French, English translation and foreign marketing should all be envisaged as a single operation and the financial viability considered as a whole. This is perfectly feasible if the work is of high quality and the publisher has drive and good connections abroad. In extreme cases, some State aid from the research budget might be envisaged, provided it is at a moderate level. Research resources should not be used to finance the dissemination of second-class work by lazy publishers.

It is important that this debate should not be clouded by partisan passions and baseless accusations which find echoes in the national press. Scientists who decide to reach the widest possible audience by putting in extra time and effort to publish their work in English are not slavishly following a trend nor are they lackeys of American imperialism. Those who express genuine concern about the future of French as a means of scientific expression are not simply failures, jealous of others, behind the times or chauvinists.

Having said this, let us not forget that in science as in everything else, what one does counts for more than the manner in which it is told, and that we shall be judged on the former rather than the latter.

Those who find *anglopük* unbearable should take heart from the example of our mathematicians who publish in French and are widely read.

The day when the development of natural science in France reaches such a high standard that no foreign scientist worthy of the name may ignore the news coming from France, the domination of English will collapse of its own accord. Let us strive for this achievement which is perhaps closer than we think, and in doing so, let us not confuse cause and effect by wasting our hard-earned but slender resources on the pursuit of false goals.

Doubts and Certitudes
of an Elderly Physicist*

Ladies and Gentlemen, Members of the International Conference of Great
Electrical Networks, do not expect to hear from me about Great Electrical
Networks, because you know about it far more than I do. I would like to
spend the best part of the next microcentury, John von Neumann's favorite
time unit, telling you about some of my doubts and certitudes drawn from
personal experiences and reflections in the course of a career which is
nearing its term. It goes without saying that this talk reflects strictly
personal views which are not necessarily shared by the organizers of this
Conference.

I have in the past, on various occasions given here and there talks of a
similar nature to various audiences. I shall take good care not to repeat
myself in this last batch.

Under the topics to which I do not intend to return comes the distrust,
or to use a much laboured expression, contestation, of science. Of what ills
has not science been accused for more than a decade! Progress of weapons
of massive destruction, development of nuclear energy, threat of the
infamous "all electric" economy.

Allow me to digress here for a moment. Ladies and Gentlemen, I am
asking you, whose impartiality is above suspicion: what is wrong with an
"all electric" economy? I was never so happy as when I replaced the oil
furnace in my little cottage by an electric one. I was a little shy of the costs
but my electrician reassured me by explaining that he had sold many of

* Opening session of the International Conference on Large Electric Systems. August 1984.

these to employees of the Electricity Board and if electricity were too expensive, would not they be the first to know *? But let us come back to the contestation of science.

It has been accused of the growing lack of humanity of our civilization, destruction of the environment, death of folklore, smothering of our instinctive and emotional impulses and God knows what else. It had become a tool of intellectual and social oppression in the hands of scientists, serving, consciously or not, the ruling powers. In short, science was in question, science was in doubt and in the past I did not hesitate to oppose to these doubts my own certitude of the greatness and the beauty of science, incomparable instrument of culture and source of material progress.

Strangely enough, today this contestation has vanished almost completely and its rebuttal become pointless. I leave to the specialists of socalled humanitarian sciences the task of explaining this eclipse. I will be content with noting that its zenith had coincided with a period of unprecedented expansion and the eclipse with a deep economic crisis. Could it be that contestation is a luxury of the fat years?

In dealing with scientific research one should always draw a line between basic and applied research, so similar at times as to be indistinguishable, and yet so different in their motivations and their philosophy. This too is a question on which I have spoken a lot. I am coming back to it now because of two recent affairs which had attracted much attention and which in my view provide a perfect illustration of this distinction.

I had contrasted, not without some exaggeration, the difference in the philosophy of the two types of researchers by attributing to them the following reactions when faced which some physical or mechanical apparatus. The applied researcher: "if it works, what do I care why". The fundamentalist: "I don't care if does not work so long as I know why."

A recent affair dealing with oil survey, still well remembered, offers a striking example of the attitude of those who care only about results. They are shown a device which "works". They test it under various conditions and each time it "works" that is it yields information that they are able to

---

* In France they pay considerably reduced rates.

check. They are told that to protect the rights of the inventors they cannot be let in on the principle of the device. On the other hand the benefits to be reaped seem enormous compared to the odds and so, although they don't have the slightest idea of the way the machine "works", the magic trick practiced on them also "works" that is, they buy a gadget which turns out to be worthless. I firmly believe that a man steeped in basic research would have found it unbearable not to understand at least the principle of the device offered to him, and the magic would not have worked on him.

The second affair, less recent, is that of the electromagnetic machine that offered a treatment of cancer (and, as a bonus, of sleeping sickness). Famous doctors and biologists declared that they had not the slightest idea of how the machine worked, that to them it was a "black box", but that they could not help witnessing spectacular improvements in the health of patients subjected to treatment. They felt it their duty to make it known, for, after all, is not humility in front of experimental facts the first and foremost virtue of the scientist?

I am not sure that I agree unconditionally. In the present case such an attitude would lead to consider as a "black box" a certain grotto in the Pyrénées * where one should also, with a scientist's humility, witness the improvement of some patients after a brief stay in the grotto.

In the present state of science, when faced with an inexplicable phenomenon, a healthy reaction is to begin by questioning its reality. It is quite true that several times in a century utterly inexplicable phenomena do occur and force us to revise our ways of thinking from top to bottom: the negative result of Michelson's experiment on the velocity of light, the spectral content of the blackbody radiation, the radioactivity, are some famous examples. But in an overwhelming majority of cases, an inexplicable phenomenon is an artefact due to a conjunction of trivial causes, what the great American physicist Isidore Rabi used to call a *schweinerei*, or else, as most likely in the two affairs cited earlier, and in the innumerable cases of psychokinesis, extra sensorial perception, flying saucers and other nonsense, the work of cranks or crooks.

I had for a while posted in my lab the following recommendation:

* The miraculous grotto of Lourdes.

"before we throw quantum mechanics into the garbage pail, let us check the fuses once more".

It is not possible to list here all the scientific and technical revolutions which in the course of this century have changed radically our way of life and our way of thinking. I would simply like to state my doubts and my certitudes with respect to a revolution which is still in progress, and whose course shows no sign of slowing down, the computer revolution.

I must admit that I speak of it as a layman. Our physicists can be divided into two distinct categories: those who know, more or less, how to use computers and those who don't. The boundary between them is easy to trace, it is an age limit, that moves forward every year by one year, and that in 1984 I would put approximately at fifty, with some dispersion on either side. If physicists who are beyond the boundary, manage to go on doing some research it is precisely because, thanks to their age, they can command the assistance of young coworkers. Need I add that such is my own position.

Let me quote some round figures relative to the last quarter of a century. For fifteen years, from 1959 to 1974, the number of circuits on a single silicon chip, which represents a fair indication of computing power, has grown steadily with remarkable regularity by a factor two every year, then every two years during the following ten years, to reach the million today. Such chips are available on the market, starting from this year, and the physical limit of the number of components is still far away. In parallel with this growth of the hardware, new concepts in software are also progressing fast.

I will not attempt to cite all the fields where computers play an important part today because it would be tantamount to listing practically all the activities of a modern society and I shall limit myself to the physical sciences.

In that field they appear traditionally on three levels. The first, classical tool of the theoretician, is the resolution of the equations of motion of physical systems, more or less complex.

The second and the third, tools of the experimentalist, are respectively the programming and control of the running of the equipment and the processing of the outgoing signals. The distinction between these two activities is not entirely clearcut, signals from the output being sometimes used for improving the control. But a new role appears on the horizon, the computer as instrument of research and discovery, so much so that some specialists of statistical mechanics and quantum theory of fields speak now of three types of physics: theoretical, experimental, and computer physics. The latter will require in the future even higher performances but above all computers designed specially for this new task of research and discovery by the physicists themselves.

It is with respect to this last use, promoted by some very brilliant minds, that I have a reaction of doubt, not to say, of rejection. I do however mistrust this reaction of mine. It is always difficult for those whom youth has abandoned to accept novelty; after all the greatest physicist of modern times, Albert Einstein, this revolutionary, this iconoclast who shattered the images of absolute time and space could never bring himself to accept the upheaval brought about by quantum mechanics in spite of the fact that he had been one of the pioneers of its early development.

If then, in spite of my doubts such is the way of the future, so be it, but tis pity. I do not care if the next world champion of chess is a computer, I could never play chess, but I had made mine the beautiful definition of Ernest Mach: "Science is economy of thought", and it would make me sad to give it up. I find some comfort in having been able to compose this talk without the help of a computer, even though the person who typed it did use one.

The evergrowing power of computers has been a source of concern for quite some time and the writers of science fiction have given free rein to their imagination in conjuring images of future societies ruled despotically by monstrous computers.

However it is amusing to notice the timorousness and indigence of imagination displayed by the best of them in front of the lightning development of real computers. Here is what the great American novelist Kurt Vonnegut says in his novel *Player Piano* about the computer dubbed EPICAC XIV which is in charge of the entire economy of the United States and whose machinery occupies thirty enormous caverns. "This vast cavern alone, the smallest of the lot, contains more vacuum tubes than there were in the State of New York before World War II". It is remarkable that this anticipation appeared in 1953, the very year when Bardeen, Brattain and Shockley went to Stockholm to fetch their prize for the transistor.

Ira Levin, the well-known author of *Rosemary's Baby*, describes thus, in another novel a monstrous computer, ruler of the world, also located underground: "rows of mammoth steel blocks set against the next and hazed with cold... How many are there?... 1240, on this level, 1240 on the next. And that's only for now; there's twice as much space cut out and waiting...".

If in this novel, published in 1970, Levin does not mention vacuum tubes, he misses the plate, so to speak, by an even wider margin: while in real life computer progress means going from components with linear dimensions of 2 microns, standard size today, to 0,2 micron, already realized in the laboratory, the novelist sees the evolution as crowding more and more steel blocks into more and more tunnels.

This lack of vision of writers of anticipations dealing with science and technology is quite general. Our molecular biologists would bestow an indulgent smile on the descriptions of the crude manipulations to which Aldous Huxley subjects the inhabitants of *Brave New World* written in 1932. And in the innumerable speculations on the death ray, supposedly a prefiguration of the laser, what writer of fiction would ever have imagined myriads of animated pictures carried by this ray along hairs of glass.

Finally, and above all, what writer in his craziest vaticinations would have dared to say before Einstein that one of a pair of twins could return from a long voyage the junior of his brother's grand-children, what writer would have dared to spite Alfred de Musset by saying before Schrödinger that a door could be open and closed at the same time?*

I would be sorely tempted to ask the writers to leave the speculations on the future of science to scientists if they too were not prone to err almost as heavily.

How many great scientists would have liked to be able to swallow back some rash words pronounced a few years earlier!

The opposition of François Arago to railways is quite forgotten. He

---

* A comedy by Alfred de Musset has the title: "A door should be open or shut".

feared that domestic animals would be frightened to death by the passage of trains; the placid interest of cattle for passing trains demonstrates that his fears were groundless.

Better known this statement of Lord Rutherford: "anyone who expects a source of power from the transformations of these atoms is talking moonshine".

No scientist says anymore: "the laser is a solution without a problem" or "so the laser is good for holography, but what is holography good for?"

The great Pauli had called stupid the experiment attempted by Otto Stern to measure the magnetic moment of the proton: "what does the dummkopf expect to find if not a nuclear Bohr magneton?" Alas Stern found a nuclear Bohr magneton times 2.8.

I shall stop this list here, the nanocenturies are running out.

Contrasting with the general shortsightedness of the "scientific" predictions of fiction writers, one is often struck by the lucid cruelty of their anticipations of the customs and structure of the societies of the future. The reason is this: these anticipations are actually a mirror, magnifying and distorting, but a mirror all the same, thrust by the writer towards the vices that beset, or at any rate, threaten the societies of today.

The nightmarish picture of the *1984* of George Orwell, published in 1950, is not an anticipation, although he himself may have thought so, but a barely exaggerated description of very real practices which did exist at the time, although not discovered until later, and which unfortunately have not disappeared.

The haters of all kinds of elitism, the sworn enemies of selective entrance examinations to the universities, those for whom any member of the university is worth any other, and any research worker, worth any other research worker, would do well to ponder over a vision of the future, conjured by Kurt Vonnegut in another of his writings :

"The year was 2081 and everybody was finally equal. Nobody was smarter than anybody else. Nobody was better looking, stronger or quicker than anybody else, thanks to the vigilance of the agents of the Handicapper General.

George, whose intelligence was above normal, was required by law to wear at all times a little mental handicap radio. Every twenty seconds or so, the transmitter would send out some sharp noise to keep people like George from taking unfair advantage of their brains...

George was watching a ballet. The ballerinas were not very good. They were burdened with bags of birdshot and the pretty ones were masked.

Nobody seeing a graceful gesture or a pretty face, would feel small and miserable."

Do not misunderstand me. Inequalities *are* an evil and their attenuation our duty and perhaps we *do* need a Handicapper General but one who instead of bowing the heads of the tall would slip a footstool under the feet of the small. If I were the Handicapper General I would begin by the beginning. I would take good care that no child enters the sixth form *, without being able to read, write and count, and this is how I would set about it. In the absurdly remote years of my own seventh form at the good old lycée Janson-de-Sailly, there were already, would you believe it, children, children from bourgeois families naturally, the only ones who went to lycées, who could barely read, write and count. For such children, the teachers organized on their own initiative, what at Janson we called "little lessons" (and not only in the seventh form). For a respectable fee, payed by the parents of the pupils of this respectable institution, the teachers kept the little dunces after class in groups of five or ten and reached without too much trouble at the end of the year the modest goals they had set for themselves. Those who were really too lazy or too stupid stayed over for a year and passed into sixth form the following year.

Nowadays there are no little lessons and nobody stays over for a second year. We know the result. I, Handicapper General, would create "little lessons", free of charge, for all those who need them. I would appeal to the generosity of the teachers to provide on their free time this extra tuition for all the children who needed it, and who in their overwhelming majority come from underprivileged families. Should this appeal fail, I would hire more teachers. Were I denied the means to do so, I would enlist the voluntary help of private individuals. I would be greatly surprised if among

---

* In France the sixth form is the first year of the secondary cycle, the seventh the last of the elementary cycle.

educated people pushed into early retirement at 55, and chafing at the bit, I could not find enough volunteers. And if the teacher's unions were to block this attempt, well, well then, a Handicapper General of the first type would replace me and everything would come back to order, the order described by Kurt Vonnegut.

Neither would I like to be taken for an unconditional supporter of unlimited selection and fierce competition. I do not believe that the atmosphere which prevails in our taupes* and among our candidates to the agregation** is a source of creative inspiration.

I remember a remark of the great violinist Isaac Stern, made after watching, during a visit to Moscow, a competition among young Soviet violinists: "Their technique is perfect but I cannot escape the impression that they play Mozart against each other." Do not our brightest candidates competing for first rank at the École Polytechnique or the Agregation, play Maxwell's equations or Cauchy's theorem against each other? Our colleagues of Oxford University anxious to humanize their procedures of admission lay great stress on the informal individual interview of each candidate with a Fellow of the College he wishes to enter. Is it surprising that some of the schools which specialize in preparation for Oxford, offer in their last form, classes of collective preparation to individual interviews with "dress rehearsals" of such interviews.

I have alluded earlier to the myopia of scientists with respect to possible applications from their own field. Here is an example which touches me closely, NMR imaging.

The acronym NMR stands for Nuclear Magnetic Resonance. It is a discipline born after the last war, whose object is the study, by means of radiofrequency techniques, of the collective behaviour of nuclear magnetic moments in bulk matter, when placed in a high magnetic field. I shall say no more about NMR; a short account aimed at the layman can be found at the beginning of this book. NMR imaging uses the methods of NMR to obtain images of human organs. It is a relatively expensive technique which

---

* Taupes: special classes preparing candidates through strenuous work to the competitive entrance examinations to prestigious *Grandes Écoles*.

** Agregation: competitive examination crowning the preparation to a teacher's career.

requires large magnets producing high very homogeneous magnetic fields over sizeable volumes and a sophisticated radioelectric equipment coupled to a prowerful computer.

Still in its infancy, unknown a few years ago, NMR imaging provides already images of a quality at least as good as the X-ray scanner and is promised to a great development.

I discovered NMR in 1950. Those who remember that Felix Bloch and Ed Purcell were awarded the Nobel Prize in 1952, for discovering it in late 1945 need not be startled. I say: "I discovered NMR in 1950" the way people say: "I discovered sex at thirty-five". This is actually how old I was when I discovered it, NMR that is, but for various reasons I could not start a laboratory of my own till 1954. From then on, for thirty years I have been immersed in NMR or, as I prefer to call it, in nuclear magnetism. Yet, if ten years ago I had been asked whether in 1984, NMR would yield images of human organs of such outstanding quality, I would probably have said no.

What is the reason for such a shortsightedness on my part, and I may add on the part of an overwhelming majority of the leaders in the field of nuclear magnetism?

For me, although I have always been far more interested in basic research than in its applications, I do not think that this is the explanation. Indeed, when back in 1957 I imagined a method of dynamic nuclear polarization in liquids, I realized immediately its potential application to very accurate measurements of the earth magnetic field and its usefulness in oil surveying or detection of metallic objects under water. Within a few weeks, with my coworkers we took on behalf of the French Atomic Energy Commission a patent for a magnetometer based on this principle, and pushed through its development by another Department. You may remember that the shipwreck of "La Méduse" was located recently by such a magnetometer near the coast of Mauritania.

But, what has made NMR imaging the beautiful technique it is today, and, as I am now convinced, an even more powerful tool for tomorrow, is something alien to the field of NMR proper, namely the fantastic increase in computing speed and power, available for the handling of a staggering amount of information. What is easy today was impossible, not to say unthinkable, ten or fifteen years ago.

As far as I can see, there has not been any major breakthrough in NMR per se, in the course of its application to imaging but this may change. One of the reasons, which in my view will in the future bring NMR imaging far ahead of X-ray imaging is its tremendous flexibility. My old friend Erwin Hahn, the discoverer of spin-echoes, a man who probably had more bright ideas in our field than anyone else, used to say: "There is nothing that nuclear spins will not do for you, as long as you treat them as human beings."

Thus, the only advice I would give to the representatives of the medical profession, users of NMR imaging, is: "do not be content with what you have got, ask for more, much more. I am sure that the best minds in our field will rise to the challenge if you manage to capture their imagination".

Finally let me ask an important question: should one plan science? When one considers the number of highly competent people who devote to this task the best of themselves, the number of meetings where it is debated, the number of inquiries that are launched, the number of forms that are filled, the number and the volume of reports that are written, if one adds the regional and national assizes of Research, these great liturgies of science where the ardour of youth mingles with the experience of maturity, united by the same ideal, could there be any doubt about the answer.

Allow me to give my own answer, frank, categorical, devoid of ambiguity: yes and no. Or rather, yes when it is absolutely necessary and with as few details as possible.

Above all abandon the pernicious conceit that planning is in itself a "good thing" like motherhood. It is nothing of the kind. There are many circumstances at least in "Little Science" where the much despised rule of thumb: "use last year's budget, give or take five percent, in real money", is as good as a detailed inventory of the goals to be reached and of the means to be procured. Most of the time this is the kind of funding that a laboratory or a group of laboratories is going to get anyway and the elaborate planning is simply a window-dressing harmful in more ways than one: submitting detailed plans that are not even read at the top is a waste of the scientist's time that would be better employed at doing research; submitting plans that *are* read may be worse because it is unnecessarily binding.

When detailed planning is an absolute necessity as in some large projects, the key word is flexibility. This concept in my view pervades not only all planning of science but the conduct of human affairs in general.

One can draw an illuminating analogy from the trajectory of a missile. It is impossible to fix exactly at the start all the parameters which govern this trajectory. It is bound to depart from the prescribed course and left to itself will never reach its target. It is essential to measure continually the departure of the missile from the prescribed trajectory and to modify its course accordingly.

In planning too, flexibility rests on the concept of feedback: to perceive as early as possible what has gone wrong and to have the means and the *will* to change the plan accordingly. This may ultimately involve giving up the project altogether if the plan reveals itself hopelessly wrong (the missile analogue would be to destroy a missile gone too far astray). It is cheaper in the long run, to scrap a bad project half-completed than to bring it to completion because so much has been invested already. Some concrete examples :

The construction of the soviet accelerator of Dubna, with an energy of 10 GeV, and with more iron than a battleship, 35,000 tons, began in 1949. It was based on the principle of so-called weak focussing, made obsolete in 1953 by the discovery a year earlier of strong focussing, which reduced the weight of iron by an order of magnitude while improving the quality of the particle beam. The first CERN synchroron based on that principle and with an energy of 26 GeV was started in 1953. The ill-conceived Dubna machine which had also other built-in defects came into operation in 1958 and never performed properly. It would probably have been wiser to scrap it half-way through completion, in 1954, and to start again with the new focussing principle rather than to burden a generation of physicists with a white elephant (or rather, considering its size, a blue whale).

The Soviet physicists, saddled with this contraption, sought relief by showering sarcasms on the enormous beast: "we have in the Kremlin the largest cannon in the world which never fired and the largest bell which

---

* Pronounced like reason.

never tolled, and also the largest accelerator..." and they defined their programme as follows: "one meson * per season". Some justified thus the enormous absurdly overestimated dimensions of the vaccuum chamber: "if we cannot get protons, we can accelerate graduate students instead". On all fours, there was room.

I remember that in 1954 I had spent two months in Geneva with Felix Bloch, the first director of CERN. His two favorite sayings were: "All theories of superconductivity are wrong and all big machines eventually work". He turned out to be wrong on both accounts. The Dubna accelerator never really worked and the theory of Bardeen, Cooper and Schriffer, which came three years later, turned out to be the right one.

The rigidities of the planning responsible for the Dubna mishap, should not obscure the prominent contribution to the development of particle accelerators from men like Veksler, inventor of the principle of synchronous acceleration, Budker, pioneer of colliding rings and many other Soviet scientists.

The French too started in 1953 a weak-focussing machine named Saturne, but with an energy of 3 GeV only. I was personally concerned with the project of Saturne and I leaned toward weak focussing because for a smaller machine the saving in the weight of iron did not make that much difference and did not warrant the risks conneted with the then largely untried method of strong-focussing. The CERN engineers had no choice. A weak focussing 26 GeV machine would have been a monster.

I take some pride in having had the guts to stop a largish project in controlled fusion, a machine called Superstator, not indeed before construction had started, but after it had been authorized, the money (40 millions francs 1968) made available, and the orders about to be passed to industry. This last-moment decision had upset the financial director of the CEA by putting his budget out of joint. It was motivated by the emergence of a new type of machine pioneered by the Russians, the Tokamak. The CEA eventually built a Tokamak instead of the Superstator. The large European machine, the JET inaugurated early this year by President Mitterrand and Queen Elizabeth, is also a Tokamak. Incidentally, the man who built JET, and earlier the first French Tokamak, Monsieur Rebut, was also in charge of the construction of the still-born Superstator. As for the man who was the first to imagine the principle of the Tokamak it was Andrei Sakharov.

Like the cobbler who ventures above the shoe, I would like to extend beyond the boundaries of the field of science the principle of feedback with its two components: perception of the effect and correction of the cause.

What is market economy if not the possibility for an enterprise to measure the quality of its products and the obligation to improve or at least to maintain that quality.

Above all, I do not imagine a sound system of government without feedback. The best plans prepared with utmost care by the best experts at the service of the ruling powers will not succeed if undesirable consequences, inevitable in any human undertaking, are not detected in time, and the measures which gave rise to them, corrected. No doubt, it is not always easy for our rulers to detect the telltale signals, amongst the noise, the sound and the fury, which rise towards them. Great is the temptation to cut off this troublesome noise which disturbs the peace. The name for it is censorship. Yes, but by suppressing the noise one suppresses the signals, above all the weakest, those that reveal a wrong course at its beginning while there is still time to set it right.

Winston Churchill is credited with saying: "Democracy is the worst system barring all others." Innumerable are the ethical arguments in defense of democracy. I would like to add the following, of a different nature: in spite of all its defects and of all its weaknesses, democracy with its built-in feedback system, is the most efficient system, the fittest for survival.

I might conclude here but I would like to add a last thought. During the student unrest of 1968 our young people said many foolish things defying common sense and even sometimes formal logic as in the famous: "it is forbidden to forbid" that would have amused Bertrand Russell. Yet there was a slogan that I liked: "All power to imagination." I would tone it down a little before offering it to you as a guiding rule in our own affairs, scientific and technical: "more power to imagination".

J. H. Van Vleck*

John Hasbrouck Van Vleck passed away in Cambridge (United States) on the 27 October 1980 at the age of 81. He was a Foreign Member of the French Académie des Sciences since 11 February 1974.

Van Vleck was rightly called the father of modern magnetism. He is the broker for the very productive marriage between quantum mechanics and magnetism. He was also one of the founding fathers of American theoretical physics. Now that we have seen the extraordinary blossoming of this subject in recent times, there is a tendency to forget that from the death of the great Willard Gibbs at the turn of the century until the doctoral thesis of Van Vleck, presented in 1922 to the Faculty of Sciences of Harvard University, American physics, represented by experimentalists like Rowland, Michelson, Wood, Pupin, Millikan and others, boasted very few publications on theoretical physics worthy of the name.

For more than fifty years after his doctoral thesis, Van Vleck has continued to make crucial contributions to all aspects of magnetism, and also to molecular physics, theoretical chemistry, radiospectroscopy, propagation of electromagnetic waves in the atmosphere and the study of the interaction of crystal or phonon vibrations with paramagnetic centres. He has been the guiding light for several generations of physicists, among whom the signatory of this obituary is happy and proud to count himself.

* Obituary for J. H. Van Vleck, Foreign Member. Read before the French *Académie des Sciences*, November 1982.

Professor at the University of Minnesota from 1923 to 1928 and then at Wisconsin from 1928 to 1934, Van Vleck returned to his alma mater, Harvard, the most prestigious of the American universities, where he passed the rest of his long career until retiring from the Hollis chair in 1969, although this did not mean his retirement from science. Among the many visiting professorships there were two of particular prestige, the Lorentz chair at the University of Leyden in 1960 and the Eastman chair at the University of Oxford in 1961.

Between 1943 and 1945 he participated in the American war effort as Director of the theoretical group of the Harvard Radiation Laboratory, created to assist the National Defense Agency in all problems relating to radar and in particular the jamming of enemy radar.

From 1945 to 1949 Van Vleck was chairman of the Department of Physics at Harvard. He attracted men who made American physics famous, such as Purcell, Schwinger, Ramsey, Pound and Bloembergen.

In 1951 he accepted the post of Dean of the Division of Engineering and Applied Physics, which had just been created. He set up a most productive symbiosis between that Division and the Physics Department, symbolized by the construction, at his initiative, of a covered bridge between the two buildings which housed the two departements. A shrewd psychologist, he could see that nothing would bring the two research groups closer in spirit than the physical proximity and the possibility of crossing from one laboratory or office to the other without having to brave the rigours of the long cold Cambridge winter.

Van Vleck's career was marked by many high honours bestowed by the scientific societies of all countries. Beside those awarded by his own country, we should mention his titles of Foreign Member of the Royal Academies of Sweden and Holland and the Royal Society of London, together with an honorary doctorate of Oxford University. Our own *Académie des Sciences* bestowed the title of Correspondant in 1960 and Foreign Member in 1974. The French Universities awarded him the Honorary Doctorates of Grenoble, Paris and Nancy, and the French Physical Society made him an Honorary Member, while the French government nominated him *Chevalier de la Légion d'Honneur*.

In 1974 he became the eleventh holder of the Lorentz Medal, following in the footsteps of Planck, Pauli and Debye; since 1927 this has been awarded every four years to a theoretical physicist by the Dutch Royal Academy. Finally in 1977, the Nobel Prize, shared with his most brilliant pupil Philip Anderson and with the British physicist Nevill Mott, was the culmination of his prestigious career, and, in the opinion of his admirers and friends, none too soon. We had the great pleasure of welcoming him to France on his way back from Stockholm, and on this occasion I had the opportunity to say a few words of welcome which I beg leave to repeat to you today.

"There are two types of Nobel laureate: those who owe a great deal to the award, which suddenly turns their notoriety into celebrity, and those to whom the Prize owes a great deal, more than it brings in return. If today, despite the existence of other prizes of equal or greater monetary value, the Nobel Prize remains the supreme accolade that scientists dream about, it is because of laureates such as John Van Vleck."

Let me now review some of the highlights of the scientific career of Van Vleck. After his doctoral thesis, devoted to the calculation of the energy of the helium atom by the old quantum theory of Bohr and Sommerfeld, and some studies on electromagnetic radiation based on Bohr's Correspondence Principle, Van Vleck became fascinated by the new quantum mechanics proposed by Dirac and Heisenberg.

As early as 1926, he decided to use these methods, which were quite revolutionary at the time, to develop the theory of magnetic susceptibility, marking the birth of modern magnetism, or at least, modern paramagnetism.

Three important articles published in 1927 and 1928 established the theory of paramagnetism in the gas phase. The first detailed application of this formalism was the prediction that NO and O_2 are paramagnetic, which was very soon confirmed by measurements performed in Leyden, M.I.T. and Zürich. Van Vleck showed the importance of excited states which lead to a temperature-independent magnetism, known in the literature as Van Vleck magnetism.

Next, Van Vleck applied quantum mechanics to the study of the rotational and vibrational spectra of diatomic and polyatomic molecules in a series of important papers spanning the years from 1928 to 1934. But from 1929 onwards he tackled the problem which he would never abandon throughout his career, the magnetic properties of the transition elements in the solid state, the iron group and the rare earth elements.

The Solvay conference in 1930 at which he was the only American participant, marked an important milestone in Van Vleck's career; he recognized the importance for the theory of magnetism of the crystal field effect in solids, and through Bethe's classic article, made himself familiar with group theory, an indispensible tool for the study of crystal field effects.

In 1932, the publication of his book, *The Theory of Electric and Magnetic Susceptibilities* established his reputation once and for all. This book has remained the key reference work for all engaged in research on magnetism for forty years, in spite of the fact that it was written too early to be able to include, except qualitatively, all the applications of crystal field theory, which in the hands of Van Vleck and his students, would play a key role in the theory of modern magnetism.

All the static properties of paramagnetic insulators are described quantitatively in agreement with experiment, based on some simple, reasonable hypotheses about the symmetry of the crystal field and the relative magnitude of its different components in comparison with the strength of the spin-orbit coupling in the magnetic ions. In this way the quite different magnetic behaviour of the iron group and the rare earths is quite naturally explained by the fact that crystal field is stronger than the spin-orbit coupling in the iron group, and weaker in the rare earth series.

Van Vleck was perfectly well aware that the description of the environment of a paramagnetic ion in terms of an electrostatic crystal field is only an approximation when there are covalent bonds between the ion and the ligands. He was able to show, using the more realistic language of molecular orbitals, that what essentially determines the magnetic behaviour of an ion is the local symmetry rather than the nature of the bonding, and that covalent bonds may be represented in terms of a strong crystal field of the right symmetry.

Along with these studies of the static magnetic properties, Van Vleck investigated the dynamic behaviour corresponding to an exchange of energy between the magnetic moments and the crystal lattice, where the lattice vibrations modulate the crystal field. He is the father of the modern theory of paramagnetic relaxation, first studied experimentally at Leyden by the school of Gorter. In his description of the direct relaxation process, that is to say, where the energy is exchanged between a magnetic moment and the lattice by means of a single photon, he proposed for the first time the concept of "phonon bottleneck", fifteen years prior to the first observation of this phenomenon.

The discovery of electron and nuclear resonance methods after the war provided the Van Vleck theories with a new and wider field of application.

In a seminal article published in 1948, he introduced a rigorous method of calculating from first principles, the various moments of the magnetic resonance lines, a method which today still remains the most reliable method of predicting the linewidths. In the same way he applied the method of moments to the quantitative description of a remarkable phenomenon—the appreciable line narrowing which occurs when there are quantum mechanical exchange (scalar) interactions between magnetic moments.

In 1939, Van Vleck participated in the Strasbourg Conference on Magnetism, and gave eight lectures in French; because of the war these conference proceedings were not published until eight years later when they appeared in 1947 in the *Annales de l'Institut Henri Poincaré*. Although little known in the English-speaking community, these conferences represent a rigourous and penetrating analysis, the finishing touch to the theory of magnetism.

During the war, as part of his duties in the Harvard radioelectrical laboratory, he gave his attention to the absorption by water vapour of electromagnetic waves used for radar, which led him to a rigorous theory of collision broadening of microwave lines in the gas phase.

His interest was aroused by many other problems thrown up by the development of radiofrequency spectroscopy. In 1952 in collaboration with the present author, he developed the theory of the Zeeman effect in atomic oxygen, taking in account the corrections due to the relativistic effects and to the finite mass of the nucleus.

The enormous breadth of Van Vleck's work in the field of paramagnetism should not be allowed to obscure the importance of his contribution to the understanding of the collective states of atomic and molecular magnetic moments, ferromagnetism, antiferromagnetism and ferrimagnetism, where our countryman Néel had long ago claimed the lion's share.

Of particular note was a penetrating explanation of the anisotropy induced in cubic crystals by anisotropic exchange interactions, together with several review articles written in the nineteen-fifties on the theory of spin waves and on the coupling of angular momentum in polyatomic molecules. These were marvels of clarity and exposition.

For many years, Van Vleck had been contemplating a new edition of his masterpiece *The Theory of Electric and Magnetic Susceptibilities*. The project was never completed, and I believe it never could be done by a single individual, even Van Vleck, because the subject had grown so much in size and importance, due, above all, to Van Vleck's own efforts.

In conclusion, there remains the task of drawing a rapid sketch of the man himself.

In order to understand the enchanting personality of Van Vleck, it is first necessary to place him in the framework of his native America. As he occasionally admitted, with some pride and a little irony, he was that rare bird, a tenth generation American. His ancestor, Tielman Van Vleck (with two e's) arrived in the town that was still called New Amsterdam in 1658. John Van Vleck's mother, née Hester Lawrence Raymond, belonged to the Raymond family which had left England for the United States at the end of the seventeenth century, and which, according to family tradition, was descended from Count Raymond of Toulouse, who was forced to seek refuge with the King of England when he was defeated by Simon de Montfort. Perhaps it is this long and glorious ancestry which explains the lifelong affection of John Van Vleck for our country, our civilization and our language, which he began to learn as a pupil in the École Alsacienne while his father was on sabbatical at the University of Paris at the turn of the century.

The connections between the Van Vleck family and the University and the exact sciences date from the time of John Van Vleck's grandfather, John Monroe Van Vleck, who was an astronomer and Professor of Mathematics at Wesleyan University in Middletown, Connecticut. John Monroe had three daughters and one son, Edward Burr Van Vleck. All four taught mathematics. Edward Burr, John Van Vleck's father, had a particularly distinguished career as mathematician since he was a member of the United States Academy of Science and had the pleasure of seeing his son as a member alongside him from 1935 to 1943. Through his ancestry and through his upbringing Van Vleck belonged to what used to be called the aristocracy: aristocracy by birth in a nation of immigrants, aristocracy in the intellectual and social sense by virtue of his family background and even more through his personal success which was precocious and brilliant. And yet I can swear that no man was more simple, approachable, and less subject to pride and vanity. He spoke with the same courtesy and in the same register to all, University President or graduate student, and he always made a point of holding the door for a lady whether she were the wife of a colleague or the office cleaner. After all, that is perhaps the true aristocracy.

In America, where it is not impolite (or at least was not impolite thirty years ago) to ask someone how much he earned and how he voted, Van Vleck never hid the fact that he supported the more conservative party, the Republicans. This did not prevent him, in contrast to some of his colleagues with more liberal ideas, to make a courageous defence of one of his Harvard colleagues, Wendell Furry, the victim of a witch-hunt organized by the Republican senator McCarthy in the nineteen-fifties.

In his professional life, he always showed great goodwill and great modesty. I never heard him express any criticism even of those colleagues who, to my certain knowledge, did not measure up to his standards. Moreover in the field of theoretical physics, where ideas circulate quite freely and where it is not always easy to identify the originator, he was most meticulous in refusing to accept the credit for work which might, in part at least, be attributed to others. He was quite put about when, in his presence, I mentioned the Van Vleck vector model, a term used by everyone, because he felt that the idea was entirely due to Dirac. His kindness and goodwill were particularly evident in his dealings with young scientists. He was never too busy to put in a word to help them get an appointement, a scholarship, accommodation or even a ticket for American football, a sport of which he was an enthusiastic supporter, particularly when his own University team was involved. As many others I often reaped the benefit of his extraordinary kindness.

Let me in conclusion repeat some of the remarks I made on the occasion of his visit to France in 1977.

A profile of Van Vleck would not be complete without mention of one innocent and charming passion, his love of railways. His competence in this field included not only an encyclopaedic knowledge of the time-tables and itineraries of all the principal railways of the world, but also the more detailed information, acquired at first hand, of their respective quality—speed, comfort, maintenance of the track, the standard of the food in the restaurant-cars and the bed-linen in the sleeping-cars. Endless stories are told about this among the friends and admirers of Van Vleck.

Thirty years ago, with his usual attention to detail, Van Vleck made the arrangements for my wife and myself to take a transcontinental train journey across the United States, which I shall always remember with great pleasure. He was quite insistent on our taking a particular train for one of the stages of the journey. When I asked if this was really a good train he replied that he would really like to know himself and was counting on me to tell him.

I would like to say in closing that to my mind John Van Vleck embodied the principal virtues (and perhaps some of the faults) of the great American nation: the love of liberty, free enterprise, hard work, kindness, generosity, courage and also simplicity and that sense of humour which ensures that you never take yourself too seriously. In the words of that familiar American expression, Van Vleck could perhaps be said to be "as American as apple pie"; I would rather say "as American as Abraham Lincoln".

It is still open for discussion whether there have been scientists more admired by their colleagues; there are none that have been more loved.

Claude Bloch*

Claude Bloch has left the mark of his immense talent on all the fields of fundamental science that have interested him, from the theory of the structure of the atomic nucleus and of nuclear reactions, the statistical mechanics of strongly interacting systems to the theory of spectral densities.

The essence of this work is its generality, its clarity, its rigour, and, despite its pioneering nature, the words "classical perfection" spring naturally to mind.

If Claude Bloch chose to take on problems that were larger, more general and (let us admit it) more abstract than those which preoccupy the experimental physicist and the engineer, it was not through disdain for practical matters, a typically French failing, even less through incapacity to deal with such problems, an even more frequent failing. In the fields of reactors and of particle accelerators, I have myself seen him solve difficult technological problems as if it were a game, where the specialist engineers were bogged down. Quite simply and naturally he chose to take on problems worthy of his intellect.

The publications of Claude Bloch form an integral part of contemporary physics, but that is far from being the sum-total of his contribution to science. An incomparable teacher, he has trained and supervised students, some of whom have themselves become research leaders. He taught them an appreciation of rigour and a contempt for hazy ideas and sloppy thin-

* Eulogy at the funeral of Professor Claude Bloch, January 1972.

king, together with a realization of the dangers inherent in excessive specialization. A man who invented and utilized the most refined mathematics with elegance and unrivalled skill, he nevertheless gave his students and collaborators a feel for practical matters, and for that constant quest for contact with physical reality and a language the experimentalist could understand.

The result was the creation of a group of theoreticians, which, for the breadth of its interests, the quality of its work and the effectiveness of its support for experiment, is second-to-none in the world.

Claude Bloch was a teacher whose name stands alongside other famous leaders like Landau, Wigner and Oppenheimer.

What can I say about this man we all knew? His natural kindness and generosity was deliberately hidden behind a certain reserve tinged with irony, and those who didn't know him well sometimes found him cold. It is true that he never tried to hide his distaste for chatterboxes, social climbers and fools, whether they had titles and honours or not.

He never expected to advance his career by anything other than the quality of his work, and all coteries and cliques, all mutual admiration societies and external marks of what is sometimes called success—medals, honorary degrees and chairmanship of committees—all left him completely indifferent.

In complete contrast, for the young scientists who came to him to learn how to do research, if they had the ability and the will to work, he had inexhaustible supplies of forbearance and patience. It was difficult to win his friendship, but once he accepted you, he was a good and faithful friend. He travelled widely and was very well read. He was highly cultured and had a wide appreciation of literature, art and music, and his lively wit made him a charming companion.

About a year ago, at the instigation of all his friends and colleagues, he accepted the post of Director of Physics of the French Atomic Energy Commission. He was an immediate success. His authority and judgement made it clear that, as many of us had suspected, there was a man of action inside the man of science.

When many of us here have passed on, the work of Claude Bloch will continue to be his memorial.

Felix Bloch *

Like his contemporaries Hans Bethe and Lev Landau, Felix Bloch arrived on the heels of the famous trio Heisenberg, Pauli and Dirac, who were separated from him by no more than a few years and who had just given the world the marvellous tool of quantum mechanics. For more than thirty years nobody used this tool with more originality, elegance or efficiency than Felix Bloch.

If the Nobel Prize that he shared with Edward Purcell in 1952 was the accolade for the great discovery (in 1946) of Nuclear Magnetic Resonance (NMR for short) or "nuclear induction" as he liked to call it, at least three other earlier discoveries might have won Bloch the same prestigious award.

The first of these discoveries was the theory of the movement of conduction electrons in metals. The successful electrical conductivity models of Drude, Lorentz and Sommerfeld, where electrons move freely as if there were no such things as immobile ions, were a mystery. In his doctoral dissertation and afterwards in an article of 1928 which became famous (his second publication, at the age of 22!), Bloch demonstrated that the presence of the ions does not inhibit the conduction electrons from propagating almost freely like a plane wave, modulated to the periodicity of the lattice. With this article he laid the foundations for an electron theory of solids not only applicable to metals but also to crystalline solids in general and in particular to semiconductors, the applications of which are of dominant importance in our present-day industrial civilization.

* Article paru dans l'*Encyclopaedia Universalis*.

Two years later in 1930 he created the theory of low-temperature ferromagnetism by showing that at such temperatures the basic excitations of a ferromagnetic system could be described as plane waves, termed "spin waves", linear superpositions of magnetic excitations located on each atom. In this way he obtained for the first time the (non-analytical) law of variation for the specific heat and magnetization of a ferromagnetic as a function of temperature in the neighbourhood of absolute zero. More generally, the theory of spin waves is the point of departure for the modern description of elementary excitations in condensed matter in the shape of quasi-particles, which Landau was to make such great use of subsequently. In the same sphere of ferromagnetism, Bloch demonstrated in 1932 that, in a ferromagnetic with domains, between two adjoining domains magnetization changes direction gradually across a kind of intervening wall which has come to be referred to as a "Bloch wall". This finding was to have spectacular application some thirty years later with NMR of the ferromagnetics.

From 1935 onwards Bloch came to have a passionate interest in the magnetic properties of the neutron: his imagination was enraptured by the very idea that a magnetic moment could exist in a neutral particle. He showed that a slow neutron beam passing through a magnetic substance polarizes and, conversely, the transmission of such a beam by a ferromagnetic is a function of its polarization. He used these ideas as the basis for the very precise resonant measurement of the magnetic moment of the neutron, carried out with Alvarez in 1939: the polarization of a neutron beam produced as it crosses an initial magnetized element or polarizer is reduced in resonant fashion by a radiofrequency field before being detected when it passes over a second magnetized element or analyzer.

Propagation of electrons in crystalline solids, spin waves and Bloch walls; magnetic interactions of slow neutrons with matter, and measurement of the magnetic moment of the neutron: these were the three great discoveries that came as precursor to NMR.

NMR, which he discovered together with Hansen and Packard in 1946, independently of and almost at the same time as the team of Purcell, Pound and Torrey, has since undergone prodigious development which continues in the present day. Its applications in numerous branches of physics, in later years in chemistry, biochemistry, biology, and now in medicine with NMR imagery, are too well-known to go into in detail here.

We will merely note that Bloch, a virtuoso of quantum mechanics, deliberately used classical language in his voyage of discovery towards NMR, in the same way as he did when describing his findings. He speaks of the precession of macroscopic nuclear magnetization and of the electro-motive force it induces in the detector coil, rather than of quantum transitions between energy levels of nuclear spins (the language used by the Purcell team), because classical language better conveys the coherence that exists between the movements of different nuclear moments.

The hallmarks of Bloch's work are elegance (he was wont to refer disapprovingly to Boltzmann's witticism "Elegance is something I leave to tailors"), together with conciseness (his works are not very numerous and with a few exceptions quite brief), and a remarkable sense of experimental realism. Bloch was apt to describe himself as an experimental physicist. If his own attempts to get actively engaged in laboratory experiments were not, in the opinions of his students, always crowned with success, he was an experimenter in a deeper sense, aware of the possibilities and limitations of experimental methods and apparatus and designing the experiments that his colleagues carried out. All his pupils, even those who had only limited contact with him, bore a deep imprint from his influence. Highly cultured, very active in outdoor pursuits, with a vigorous sense of humour, although impatient when it came to stupidity, Felix Bloch was a charming companion.

In the age of the computer, when experimental techniques are dominated by the accumulation of data and theoretical techniques by the accumulation of numerical calculations, a whole style of physics based on simplicity and clarity was taken from us with the death of Felix Bloch.

Mobility in Fundamental Research*

I would like to avoid any misunderstanding and make it quite clear that my idea is not to move men, let alone teams of scientists, from some activity which we would like to curtail into some other area which we would like to develop. A "recycling" of this kind can sometimes be useful and even necessary, but that is not the question here. In the experiment I have in mind, the reassignment of a certain number of physicists, even if it left the average manpower of every research unit unchanged, would still have an overall positive effect.

Many of us came into our present fields of research not by rational choice but through secondary considerations—the example of a friend, the stimulation of a particular course of study or the negative influence of an exacting series of lectures, whether the laboratory was conveniently near to home, or because we knew the head of the laboratory personally. The author himself decided on magnetic resonance rather than quantum field theory because he found the city of Oxford more attractive than Birmingham! Such decisions are perhaps no less valid than those made after long hours of heart-searching, but it may well be asked whether a physicist who chooses his career at 24, should necessarily stay in the same rut (or plough the same furrow, if you like) right up to retirement. I feel there are many things to be said for a change.

You know as well as I that one of the dangers to which a research

* Letter written by the Director of the Physics Division of the French Atomic Energy Commission to the Heads of all Physics Departments of the Division, 29 September 1970.

scientist is prone is disenchantment—a tendency to become blasé. In his career he might bring off four or five original experiments or theoretical investigations, and it is hard to raise the same enthusiasm and excitement at the idea of undertaking just one more. This is to the detriment of science, for this new piece of work could be just as important as the preceeding ones. The point of attracting new doctoral or postdoctoral candidates into the laboratory is not merely to keep the research going and to replace those who retire. It is above all because these young scientists find their first problems fresh and exciting and they give their best, their relative inexperience being more than compensated by the joy of discovery.

A scientist who has made a name in one subject and who then takes on a different area, may rediscover his early enthusiasm that had begun to lose its sparkle over the years. The result is a fuller scientific life for him and increased effectiveness in his research, a double advantage.

There is another advantage which is perhaps even more interesting. An experienced research scientist who takes on a new field does not arrive empty-handed. He already possesses the concepts, the way of thinking, methodology and techniques which allow him to attack new problems in a way which may seem original to the personnel in his new laboratory. Such a cross-fertilization bodes well for the progress of science.

Finally, there is that self-confidence and self-esteem felt by a physicist who makes such a transition between fields. The main reason for staying in a given field and the dread of changing direction, particularly into applied research or into industry, is the feeling that the hard-won knowledge and techniques might be wasted in a new field of research requiring different kinds of knowledge, even different personal qualities.

If he can convince himself and others that such a transition can be accomplished, under conditions which we should examine very carefully, and after prior examination of the problems, with our support during the transition, and with the possibility of reversion to the original post if it does not work out as he had hoped, then he will not be afraid to make other changes in the future, however radical, and will feel the master of his own destiny.

Finally, although there is no guarantee that such an experiment should succeed in the Division of Physics, it seems to me that our organization is one that is most likely to provide the best chances of success.

In this utopian description I have only presented the advantages of the proposal; there are of course several drawbacks.

The most obvious is a temporary loss of efficiency. Its duration, severity and long-term consequences can only be judged by experience. If mobility becomes widespread, there is even a danger of disorganizing our research teams and scientific investigations already under way. I believe there is really not much danger of this happening. I am more concerned about the opposite situation where nothing happens, where everyone is busy encouraging someone else to try a change (just what I am now doing myself).

In fact, if it turns out that the end result of all these individual changes of direction makes itself felt as a net gain for one discipline at the expense of another, that should be recognized for what it is and the corresponding lessons learnt about the directions of our research.

The practical details of how such a reorganization might be accomplished need considerable thought. I will leave the details to your colleagues, and restrict my remarks to some quite general comments.

Every physicist who contemplates a change of field should expect to find in his proposed new research group, sufficient information to allow him to make his decision. Each group should have someone responsible for seeing that this information is available. This information might be handled at several levels—at the beginning, a general introduction, then more and more detail according to the interest expressed by the physicist as he becomes more committed to the change. Then comes the initiation, each candidate should have one or two "godfathers" in the new group to keep an eye on him. Then there would be a trial period after which the physicist would either confirm his decision to change laboratories or return to his original group. No administrative changes would be made until it became clear that the move had been a success.

You know of our work in particle physics, nuclear physics, plasma physics, solid-state physics, atomic physics and theoretical physics. I believe this range is wide enough, and that our laboratories are sufficiently competitive with other laboratories at home and abroad that there would be no need for these exchanges to go outside the Atomic Energy Commission, at least in the first instance. The advantages are obvious. By keeping the operation "in house" we can more easily organize the procedure—information, welcoming the newcomer, initiation, trial period, the possible return to the original group—indeed all the necessary precautions to make the experiment most likely to succeed.

A change of field by moving to a laboratory outside the Atomic Energy Commission would of course be arranged in the same way as in the past, for those who wished to do this.

I hope that the principle and eventually the practical details of this experiment will be considered and discussed between you and the physicists involved, through the appropriate committees. While I feel it is a good idea, it is really a question for you and your coworkers to decide if it is really feasible. You can lead the horse to water, but you cannot make him drink.

Return to the Fold*

As head of department since 1959 and director of the Physics Division since 1965, I have divided my time between the duties of administrator and the activities of research and teaching. Without wishing to boast, I think I can say that with a sustained effort I have managed so far to avoid failure in both activities.

You know the accomplishments and successes of the Physics Division. Through the efforts and talents of my colleagues, group leaders, physicists, engineers and technicians, thanks to their confidence in me and thanks of course to the equipment put at their disposal, the record of the Physics Division has made it one of the very top laboratories for fundamental research in the world.

On the other hand, on a personal note, the scientific community, both at home and abroad, has accorded me several tokens of recognition of my recent work, these last few years, which have persuaded me that it is not yet time to retire from physics.

Now it grieves me to admit that because of the pressure on my time, I can no longer be sure to maintain the proper balance between my own work and the more and more demanding responsibilities of my administrative duties. On the other hand, I am convinced that only an active physicist can effectively carry out the duties of coordination and administration inherent in this post. The confidence of my colleagues and my authority over them

* Letter to the Head of the French Atomic Energy Commission, 13 November 1970.

would soon evaporate if I lost the ability to understand and appreciate their work and their experiments.

To continue under such conditions would be equivalent to becoming a second-rate physicist and a second-class research director. Five years as head of physics is a sufficiently long stint. It is, I think, a wise move, and perhaps a good example to others for me to pass my responsibilities on to a colleague in order to devote my energies completely to research in the magnetic resonance laboratory which I built fifteen years ago, and which I think has need of me in the same way as I need it.

I would like to ask your leave to resign my responsibilities as head of physics in order to devote myself to leading the research group in magnetic resonance at the laboratories of the Centre d'Etudes Nucléaires, Orme des Merisiers.

On the Subject of Y. Orlov and A. Sakharov*

I have decided to resign as vice-president of the International Union of Pure and Applied Physics. Naturally, I owe you and the members of the executive committee an explanation for this decision.

Together with many of my colleagues in physics, I was profoundly shocked by the treatment which the government of the Soviet Union has inflicted on certain scientists, and in particular the two physicists Yuri Orlov and Andrei Sakharov.

After many protests to no avail, a large number of physicists, of whom I am one, came to the conclusion that it was necessary to demonstrate even more vigorously that we were in fundamental disagreement with this treatment, and to boycott for the time being, all official relations with the representatives of Soviet science.

This has been a very painful decision for me because I have great esteem and even admiration for Soviet science; some of their scientists have been very old friends. However I am convinced that my course of action is in the best long-term interests of the Soviet scientists themselves, for science can not prosper in shackles.

I am aware that certain eminent colleagues do not share this point of view and have expressed themselves publicly in this vein. It appears to me that this is a problem where each man should make up his mind according to his own conscience if he is lucky enough to live in a free country.

---

* Letter to L. Kerwin, Secretary General, resigning the Vice-Presidency of the International Union of Pure and Applied Physics, July 1980.

However it seems to me that as Vice-President of the International Union of Pure and Applied Physics, I might be thought, in some circles, to be speaking on behalf of this organization if I expressed my own personal beliefs. I therefore felt it would be preferable to free myself from these ties by ending my Vice-Presidency. I hasten to add that this resignation in no way implies any disapproval of the actions of I.U.P.A.P. which I still consider to be vital for the progress of science. Moreover, as Secretary General, you know better than anyone that a Vice-President is elected *ad hominem* and that my decision in no way involves my country.

Festschrifts*

September 1967.

Dear Professor Goudsmit,

I cannot imagine how I came to miss your remarks on Festschriften, considering that your editorials are about the only thing I read in *Physical Review Letters*.

I can only hope that you will follow the French adage: "Si tu n'aimes pas cela n'en dégoûte pas les autres", and will not discourage your colleagues from participating. After all, we could devote a Festschrift to *you*.

I think you are definitely wrong when you describe Festschriften as an outlet for second-class papers by first-class authors.

There will be a second-class paper by a *second*-class author in *our* volume. I will see to it personally.

---

* Professor Goudsmit had declined to take part in a Festschrift for Professor Kastler, edited by A. Abragam, by quoting some remarks published by him in an editorial in *Physical Review Letters*.

Particle Play*

January 1982.

Dear Professor Polkinghorne,

I hope I may still address you thus in spite of the last act of the Particle Play.

I am writing to tell you that I have just finished your book and that I am still "sous le charme" (no bad pun intended in this gallicism surely permissible to a French professor).

Although, as the awful saying goes, some of my best friends are Particle Physicists, I never had the pleasure of meeting you. It is hard to imagine that a man studying for ordination to the Anglican priesthood would bear any resemblance to the fat knight and yet this phrase of Sir John irresistibly comes to mind: "I am not only witty in myself but the cause that the wit is in other men." Having read your book I feel that some of your wit (and wisdom) has rubbed off on me and that for me the great Particle Play is not any more the tale told by an idiot, full of sound and fury, signifying nothing, that it once was. My own field of physics is as remote from yours as can be. The main object of study in my laboratory is nuclear ferromagnetism and antiferromagnetism. The relevant transition temperatures are in the microkelvin range and the corresponding energies are smaller than 10^{-10} ev. Still, by and large, I did know most of the matter contained in your book, but having it retold to me in your way was sheer

---

* A book by Professor Polkinghorne.

delight. Let me thank you for the marvellous weekend I spent in your company.

Will you pardon two small remarks of a rather different nature (from each other).

It seems to me that in "Stage Machinery" you could have devoted a few lines to explaining *why* there is such a large gain in energy in going from a fixed target to colliding beams. A layman naturally expects this gain to be the same as for, say, two cars colliding head-on, namely a factor of two and your statement of a much larger gain in the ISR * is likely to puzzle him. It seems to me that by saying that in a fixed target collision, the incoming, extremely relativistic particle appears as a heavy billiard ball, hitting a pea, you would have made it clear that this mode is wasteful of energy.

On page 103 you comment not only on the American choice, but also on the American spelling of the word colour. Is it not how St. Augustine would have spelt it? I hate nite and thru but I like color (and honor).

Thanking you again for the pleasure and the enlightenment you gave me, veuillez agréer, Monsieur le Professeur et cher Collègue, l'expression de ma haute considération et de mes sentiments profondément dévoués.

---

* ISR stands for Intersecting Storage Rings.

Proposals for Experiments*

Dear Professor Goudsmit,

I wish to thank you for letting me have the comments of the referee which led to the rejection of my letter, "Possibility of Observing Cooperative Phenomena in Nuclear Magnetism" which I shall publish elsewhere.

I would like to make a few comments on those of the referee. It is naturally difficult to refute a statement, such as: "your speculations have occurred to many people". All I can say is that I have discussed the subject with leading physicists actively engaged in this field of research who did not feel that this proposal was trivial, and agreed that is was realistic and contained many ideas new to them.

However, you are probably used to such remarks from disgruntled authors and I would rather discuss a more general issue raised by the referee.

True, I do happen to lead what the referee has the kindness to call a very fine group, and they are working on the experimental aspects of this problem. However, what is the theoretical physicist to do who happens to have what he believes to be a new and realistic idea for an important experiment and who does not have an experimental group at his disposal? Is he to write private letters to various laboratories begging them to do the experiment?

I do not agree that an idea for new experiments should not be published without an experimental test. I do not believe that Gorter and Rose,

* Letter to Professor S. A. Goudsmit, Editor in chief of *Physical Review Letters*, May 1960.

Bleaney, Pound, Overhauser, to quote but a few, were wrong in making their proposals for nuclear polarization long before the experiment could be performed. I think Bloembergen was right in publishing his proposal for a three level maser, and Kastler his for optical pumping, before the experiments were done. I think Lee and Yang were right in publishing their suggested experiment on non-conservation of parity before the experiment was actually done.

If you deem it fitting to communicate these remarks to the referee I have no objection.

The Writing on the Wall

LETTER FROM PROFESSOR GINSBURG*

May 1964

It may interest you to learn that in the main lecture hall of our new Chemistry Building we are planning to cover the wall behind the lecturer with facsimile signatures of great chemists who have made important contributions to various fields of chemistry. I am sending out this letter to about one hundred chemists the world over asking for a facsimile signature. We then intend to add about 2-3 additional names annually to this chemical hall of fame.

We should be honored if you would be kind enough to send us a facsimile of your signature, written on ordinary paper *with a thick pen* and about *twice the size* of your usual signature. Our students will then be in the fortunate position of learning, also by this means, the names of the leaders of chemistry in the world today.

REPLY TO PROFESSOR GINSBURG

May 1964

Dear Professor Ginsburg,

Your very kind proposal to have my name on a wall as a great chemist demonstrates that either you do not know me or that I do not know what a chemist is. My ignorance of chemistry makes me a laughing stock among my young collaborators and if the gravity of your functions did not put you above suspicion I would have suspected that someone was pulling my leg.

If you define chemistry as the study of properties of matter in bulk I might perhaps qualify as a chemist but is not that a little farfetched? However if in the light of what I have said you still wish to keep me on your wall here is my signature more than life-size.

---

* Chairman of the Chemistry Department, Israel Institute of Technology, Haifa.